Essays in American Public Safety and Emergency Management

Essays in American Public Safety
and Emergency Management

Library of Congress Cataloging-in-Publication Data

ISBN-10: 978-1-716-47630-3

First Edition: (October 2020) (c)

10 9 8 7 6 5 4 3 2 1

Printed in the United States of America

Preface

For the most part, these papers were prepared prior to the COVID-19 Pandemic. This ironically includes my thesis on trust as a key factor for a government's efficaciousness in response to a national emergency. The premise of that work was to demonstrate, that when citizens trust their government, government is increasingly effective; and when citizens are disdainful of government, citizens can impede progress. The scenario given, was during or immediately after a national emergency or significant crisis, such as a pandemic.

In a pandemic, or other emergency, citizens must comply quickly to help their community and nation stabilize an unstable situation. During the course of that research, I coined the term *Public-Government Trust Dynamic*, this is a meaningful bond between the people and their government where both sides can profit from positive outcomes, through a symbiotic relationship which society as a whole benefits from. The Public-Government Trust Dynamic is robust when both sides accept a position where they continually seek intrinsic positive outcomes based on factors such as peace and order for society. However, when either of these two entities violate the dynamic, the arrangement fails, and it is to the detriment of both parties.

Members of society support their government by contributing to the collective pool of taxes, following the rule of law, and in times of emergencies, abiding by temporary (and often unpopular) guidelines and regulations which will help contribute to the greater good of the population. Concurrently, government aims to provide a lawful and just society, one which has the capability to properly deal with an emergency and subsequently return society to a place of equilibrium.

Public Safety personnel with proper education, training resources, and a bit of wisdom, can do wonders to help before, during and after a disaster or other emergency. They can help recovery and built resiliency for the future. Yet, those who do this job are a rare breed. Mark Twain once quipped, *"I have never let my schooling interfere with my education."* When it comes to working in public safety and emergency management, there is no classroom education which can properly and wholly prepare you for such a career field. It is my personal belief, that proficiency is best achieved by working in the field, seeing what there is to be seen, interacting with others, and absorbing wisdom from those who have developed it over time. Formal and technical education certainly helps, and there is a place for it and a high value to it—but life experiences, challenges, and life's adventures, help solidify one and best prepare him for the role. It's my hope the next generation of young people going into a career in public safety, see the value of the Public-Government Trust Dynamic, and desire to perpetuate its advancement.

The following are a collection of essays, some published, some not, all prepared between 2015 and 2020. They touch on a myriad of topics, all with an essence of public safety, and some focusing more particularly on emergency management, a passion of mine.

I would like to acknowledge an esteemed colleague and dear friend for her continued assistance, Prof. Yael Kassorla, Ph.D. Yael has been and continues to be, my occasional editor, philosophical life advisor, source of perpetual personal inspiration, confidant, and one of my best beloved friends. *You rock!*

I also could not release this work without acknowledging Jennifer, who started it all with a 'business question,' the very day I coincidently completed this book. *Wow.*

This book is dedicated to my brother, the Gunny

semper fidelis

Contents

"Day by day, what you choose, what you think, and what you do is who you become."

Heraclitus of Ephesus c.500 BCE

The Emergent Profession of Corporate Emergency Management

✿ ✿ ✿

The professional emergency manager ensures that local government and municipalities are prepared for emergencies. They seek to efficiently coordinate emergency response and recovery, and they help prepare their communities before, during, and after emergencies through preparedness, education, and response. After many decades, the profession of Emergency Management (EM) seems to have matured, and it has become a respected calling; not just across state and local governments, but throughout corporate America.

Generally speaking, a government emergency manager must be prepared and ready to respond to any type of situation, whether it is natural or man-made that effects his community. In the corporate world, emergency managers aim to be prepared for the same situations, as well as the specific interests to their businesses—such as taking actions to reduce physical infrastructure damage, minimize pecuniary losses, and mitigate injuries to employees and customers on corporate property.

Emergency Management is Born

In 1940 as war was ramping up in Europe, President Roosevelt established by Executive Order the Office of Emergency Management inside his own Executive Office of the President. This new organization helped coordinate and direct the many new civil defense and emergency preparedness organizations that were being established, in the event the U.S. would be drawn into the war. In the quarter-century following the war, to the mid-70's, if a municipality had an unusual or major emergency, it was generally established that the local fire or police chief would handle the situation. About this time, the National Governor's Association was calling for the White House to consolidate the numerous federal bodies that were responsible for various disaster-response activities. This came to fruition in 1979, when President Carter merged the existing civil defense authorities into a new organization, the Federal Emergency Management Agency (FEMA). The development of FEMA galvanized state and city governments across America to take ownership and professionalize their preparedness and response capabilities, from this came the various state and local offices of emergency preparedness / management. After the September 11

"The development of FEMA galvanized state and city governments across America to take ownership and professionalize their preparedness and response capabilities..."

attacks, the concept of civil defense was revisited under the umbrella term of "homeland security" and the "all-hazards" approach to emergency management would become a standard practice.

Emergency Management Flourishes

As the profession of Emergency Management matures, we see municipal departments of emergency management (both large and small) grow and evolve. For example, over the last couple years, New York City's 'Office of Emergency Management,' has rebranded itself, even dropping the ever-popular acronym,

'OEM.' Today, they are known as 'New York City Emergency Management' (NYCEM). They did this as part of an effort to increase the public's awareness of their role, and to elevate their office and staff's position among the professional emergency responders in New York. NYC never had an "Office of the Fire Department" or "Office of the Police Department," these were foremost city departments—not an office…of something. Today, NYCEM (with their 200+ staff) is out there 24/7 with the other primary city responders, the NYPD and FDNY. Just like in other cities, NYC's emergency management staff handles training, preparedness, mitigation, and response, as well as manages inter-agency coordination—leaving the NYPD to conduct law enforcement operations, and the FDNY to conduct firefighting operations.

Traditionally, hospitals never sought to hire emergency managers. Generally speaking, the managing of emergency's fell onto an impromptu collective of administrative and medical staff, or a management employee such as the hospital Risk Manager. The latter, of course, because one of the primary natural roles of both the Risk Manager and the emergency manager, is the mitigation of risk. Yet, if you conduct a job recruitment search today, you'll find hospitals and medical centers across the country actively seeking to hire EM personnel, especially in larger cities such as New York, St. Louis, Denver, Chicago, Austin, Washington D.C., Miami, etc.

Outside of hospitals and medical centers which are obviously reasonable places to hire an emergency manager—corporate America seems to be onboard with this trend. As of this writing, Target, Wal-Mart, Boeing, Walt Disney and Tesla are all hiring EM staff. IBM led the way some time back, incorporating an emergency preparedness role into their Real Estate and Site Operations teams which includes security staff (physical security, information security, etc.) combined with an emergency response staff person, which is a good composite for their large facilities, some that have thousands of employees. Many times, corporations are unfamiliar with the role of emergency management and what a person filling that position can do for their facility. Most understand the basics, that an emergency manager can help them plan for both potential and unforeseen emergencies, and that they have a role in hazard mitigation for the business. For this reason, emergency management staff are often hired as outside consultants, and work in symbiosis with corporations. The leading recruitment sites, LinkedIn, Monster, and Indeed, all demonstrate consulting firms looking for candidates with the International Association of Emergency Managers' credential of Certified Emergency Manager (CEM), or similar.

Corporate Emergency Management

Today, a business needs to have a preparedness program that addresses the impact of many hazards, from a fire, flood, medical emergency, to evacuation, data breach, or even dealing with an active assailant. Having a qualified emergency manager who develops a robust emergency action plan and who can train and facilitate dealing with various situations can be an advantage, because a disrupted business is one that is losing money; and lost revenues plus extra expenses means reduced profits. Further, there is the consideration of mitigating risk liability, by having a plan that deals with both employees and customers on the property of a business. An emergency action plan, a hazard reduction plan, a business continuity plan, and many others, all work to mitigate business loss and increase business resiliency. Educating senior staff, especially for large corporations, on how to use tools such as the National Incident Management System (NIMS), can be extremely helpful during an incident.

The emergency manager does not replace or supersede the corporate security staff in a large firm, but he can play a symbiotic role, dealing with the modern concerns of the corporation. The senior security professionals must focus on officer coordination, surveillance cameras, access control and entry systems, internal theft, trespassers, potentially violent individuals, investigations, liaison with the local police, etc. The emergency manager of a corporation will assist in evacuations, fire safety plans, and other plans for life safety. He will conduct vulnerability studies for the company, and educate the junior and senior staff on how to handle an emergency, or how to deal with the media and others during an incident. The emergency manager may teach incident management courses, conduct emergency exercises and drills, or tabletop exercises for executive and key personnel. Corporate EM staff are the primary liaison to the local fire department, emergency medical services, gas and electric utility companies. EM staff may work alone, or in tandem with corporate security staff to teach drills on how to handle an active assailant, or other matters of joint interest.

Emergency management personnel are those who have not only years of field experience dealing with real-life emergency situations, but also years of well-developed leadership and management skills. The professional emergency manager may have come from the fire service, law enforcement, or the military. The truth is, working in EM is never a first career for anyone. Time on the job, experience, leadership, and maturity, are all virtues of a successful emergency manager. In this day and age where corporate America faces an intrusion of violence, increasingly having to respond to unusual and unplanned situations ranging the gap from fires to cyber security emergencies to violence, bringing an emergency management staffer on board is a judicious and sensible plan.

The Evolution of Emergency Management Over the Last 25 Years

✧ ✧ ✧

In the United States, the emergency management sector of government has evolved over the last 70 years. Post-war emergency management was mostly civil defense preparedness. However, over subsequent decades emergency management has grown and advanced, and specifically over the last 25 years has matured into a very respectable profession, one that has the ability to positively impact millions of people after a national tragedy. These last 25 years have seen forward momentum that stands to carry an increasingly ready and developed emergency management through for at least the next quarter-century. As a public administrative sector which exists among the local, State and federal governments, today's, emergency managers interact with multiple stakeholders and decision-makers, and this includes politicians. General speaking, it has been the major events (disasters and other incidents) which have brought about change in public policy related to emergency management. This paper will demonstrate where emergency management has come from over the last quarter-century, and what has changed it as it matures and becomes more refined, on both the operational and legislative sides.

FEMA is Created

Modern emergency management developed out of post-World War II civil defense preparedness and readiness. There were many different civil defense organizations and agencies launched by the federal government between 1950 and 1970, many of them were conducting redundant missions. By the end of the 1970's, President Jimmy Carter, with the support of many Governors across the United States, signed an Executive Order creating the Federal Emergency Management agency (FEMA) (E.O. 12127, 1979). The introduction of FEMA was a large stepping stone for the United States in disaster preparedness. FEMA had its ups and downs over its subsequent next two decades, and a poor response to Hurricane Andrew in 1992, put FEMA under a spotlight it didn't want to be under. However, major changes came 25 years ago in 1993 right after Hurricane Andrew. Those changes had constructive ramifications which have lasted to this day. One could say that over the last 25 years, America's response to emergencies and disasters have become more streamlined, more legislatively healthy, and better than they've ever been.

The Cyclone that Was Hurricane Andrew

Towards the late summer of 1992, an Atlantic hurricane was rapidly heading towards the United States. Named Andrew, this Category 5 peak hurricane would cause >$27 billion dollars in damage and kill >60 people. The hurricane affected commercial establishments, residential areas, and military facilities across the southern US, and while the concentration of damages and loss were in Florida and Louisiana, other states including Georgia,

South Carolina, North Carolina, Tennessee, and still others, were affected by this storm; literally millions of people were made homeless by the devastation. Hearings which took place the year after Hurricane Andrew arrived. Congress criticized FEMA as did many State politicians. At the time, FEMA was still dealing with fallout from previous disasters such as Hurricane Hugo and the Loma Prieta Earthquake which left FEMA looking bad in the eyes of the public. This time around, the politicians would once again rally against FEMA, some of them lamenting: "FEMA currently lacks an effective strategy for rapid federal response…," "FEMA has not developed operating procedures to specifically guide how the federal government will provide mass care and other relief services…," and "The federal government needs to develop a catastrophic disaster response capability" (GAO, 1993, p.g. 6).

The Catalyst that Was Hurricane Andrew

The federal government, as well as state governments, have relied on national plans / guides which offer a logical but often incomplete system for responding to disasters. In 1992, just months prior to Hurricane Andrew, FEMA issued the *Federal Response Plan,* this book provided "…The mechanism for coordinating delivery of Federal assistance and resources…" to states after a major emergency. Until the attacks of September 11, 2001, this guide would be the de facto plan for dealing with a national disaster or other emergency. Still, the FRP needed improvement, and it received that after Hurricane Andrew. With the passing of the *Homeland Security Act of 2002,* the existing federal guides to how the country would react to a national emergency would be mandated to be changed into a single coordinated plan, witness the birth of the *National Response Plan*. The NRP was a rewrite of the earlier *Federal Response Plan*, but included more information and streamlined other information. It also took into effect, President Bush's *Homeland Security Presidential Directive No. 5* which mandated that the U.S. prepares for an all-hazard approach to disasters, as well as how to recover from incidents.

Another major change that came post-Andrew with the *National Response Plan,* was the use of the National Incident Management System (NIMS). This is a type of incident management system which utilizes a simple and common set of communications (FEMA, 2004). This program, which is scalable and could be used in a small events or at large events, originated with the California fire-fighting system (Klaene, 2016, p.g. 4). Made to be used generically with any type of incident, NIMS provides a framework of communications that could be used universally. The program received a lot of criticism by fire departments, police departments, and others, yet today, NIMS has been accepted, and is utilized by a majority of public safety agencies across the country. It is also used by hospitals and medical centers, corporate America, and by volunteer organizations. By utilizing the system, when everybody arrives on scene, (and depending on how well they are trained), everybody speaks the same language and can understand how the incident will be conducted. President Bush's mandate through his Presidential Directive instituted that NIMS be part of the National Response Plan (HSPD, 2003). Further, the Federal Emergency Management Agency, mandated that if your non-profit organization, or public safety organization desired to get a financial preparedness grant, all of your staff have to be trained in the National Incident Management System (FEMA, 2018). Today, NIMS classes are available online and are taught across the United States through a FEMA educational network, which is available at no charge.

It wasn't only federal changes, but new permanent implementations were established at the state level as well; these included:

- State building codes would now mandate improved structural resilience (O'Connor, 2017).
- State legislation would now mandate generators at gas stations & hospitals (F. S. 526.143).
- State and local emergency response teams were created (FEMA, 2005).

The political hearings which took place 25 years ago after Hurricane Andrew, set in motion several changes which would actually improve the Federal Emergency Management Agency, and emergency management in general across the United States. Further changes would be implemented as the years went on, and subsequent disasters continued to mar the country.

The 1994 Northridge Earthquake

The 1994 Northridge Earthquake was a 6.7 seismic event which killed >70 people and injured ~9,000. The damages of this quake surpassed $20 billion dollars, as it shook down and destroyed homes, businesses and freeways. As Andrew was an impetus for advanced hurricane forecasting, the 1994 Northridge Earthquake was the same for future seismic studies. The reauthorized of the Earthquake Hazards Reduction Act in 2004

(P.L. 108-360), directed increased research into earthquakes; it also outlined how new earthquake designs can help structures to be increasingly resilient and survive intact. A specific project was funded by FEMA, it examined earthquake hazards posed by "steel moment-resisting frame buildings" (Mahin, 1998, p.g. 261). The news media, the public, and the politicians were not so critical of FEMA during this event, as they responded rapidly and did the best they could. Years later, the country continues to become increasingly resilient due to research that yielded information from studies conducted after the Northridge earthquakes.

Hurricane Katrina

After a series of four large hurricanes striking Florida in one year (2004), Hurricane Katrina made landfall in 2005 along the Gulf of Mexico. It did catastrophic damage and displaced more than 1 million U.S. citizens from their homes. The images of the storm surge that affected the Gulf Coast looked like the ocean had entered into suburbia. That storm surge filled up homes, sending people to their second and sometimes third floors—some of the surge reaching near 30 feet I urban areas. Entire neighborhoods were under water, and the associated wind damage caused torrential damage. "I can only imagine that this is what Hiroshima looked like 60 years ago" said Haley Barbour, the exasperated Mississippi Governor upon flying over the devastation (Burdeau & A.P., 2015, p.g. 40).

During the rescue and recovery process, the Federal Emergency Management Agency was met with criticism—criticism that was presented on live television almost 24/7, for a few weeks. The media covered this story all night long, showing dramatic and highly emotional raw footage of people standing around, having no where to go, screaming into the broadcast cameras that there were rapes going on, looting, and that there was no food. The images from the Superdome (which was used as an impromptu shelter) were particularly jarring. Not to mention the panic-stricken national news reporters who shouted outrageous non-verified things on live television: "Dead people are laying around the walls of the convention center" said an MSNBC reporter (Zumbado, 2005). "[Citizens] got locked in there [by the government at the Superdome] and they watched people being killed around them, and they watched people starving…" (Smith, 2005). Whether an accurate depiction of the truth came out or not, through these reporters, the media certainly put the country into a panic. Live helicopter news broadcasts showing people stranded and sobbing on top of structures, or obviously dead bodies floating amid the dishevelled flood waters exacerbated the terror.

At the time, while the head of the U.S. Department of Homeland Security was admitting that this catastrophe exceeded the foresight of FEMA's disaster planners, the Director of the New Orleans state Department of Homeland Security was blaming FEMA. "FEMA has been here for three days, yet there is no command and control. We can send massive amounts of aid to tsunami victims, but we can't bail out the City of New Orleans" (White & Whoriskey, 2005).

Katrina Fallout

Without question, Hurricane Katrina resulted in more Congressional hearings, public townhalls, and inter-agency meetings among officials than any other natural disaster. The recovery effort was massive, and involved every governor of every state in the Union, with a large majority of them settling now-homeless refugees (FEMA, 2016, p.g. 11). The response from FEMA was unparallel and massive, yet their response was not up to par according to both the public and the politicians. The *Final Report of the Select Bipartisan Committee* that investigated Hurricane Katrina found multiple failures, at all levels of response, including technical, operational, and administrative failures. Among the latter, entire agencies did not know who they reported to during this event, including the National Disaster Medical System (NDMS), which is a joint effort between the U.S. Department of Health and Human Services, FEMA, and the V.A. (Congress, 2006, p.g. 269). The Congressmen went back and forth with FEMA representatives and FEMA blamed some of its failures on a weakened organization which was divided up after they were organized under DHS. After the Congressional activity ended, the *Post Katrina Emergency Reform Act of 2006* (PKEMRA) was enacted. This once again brought together disaster preparedness, response, and recovery programs. The PKEMRA mandated many changes and:

> The Agency became a stand-alone element within DHS, no longer characterized as the department's Directorate of Emergency Preparedness and Response. FEMA's top official became the principal advisor to the President, the

Homeland Security Council, and the secretary of Homeland Security on all emergency management-related matters in the United States. (FEMA, 2016, p.g. 12)

Additionally, a slew of operational and administrative changes affecting disaster response were put into place. These had the effect of bettering emergency management across the entire federal government, including State and local governments.

Katrina Changes

National emergency management doctrine evolved after Katrina, with the development of a new national guide, the National Response Framework (NRF), still used today, superseded the problematic National Response Plan that went into effect prior to Katrina. The NRF has an extensive system of annexes, that list critical supply and mission areas, known as Emergency Support Functions (ESF), which task various agencies during a disaster. For example, ESF#1 is responsible for Transportation, ESF#2 is Communications, ESF#3 is Engineering, ESF#4 is Firefighting, etc. The new NRF establishes an all-hazards approach to domestic incident response, including natural disasters, technological accidents and terrorist related incidents.

One of things found by Congress was that early deployment of physical and human resources was key to being ready during a disaster. When Katrina hit, FEMA was restricted to only responding after a State had made a formal request for assistance (GAO, 1993, p.g. 6); this had resulted in a deficit when it came to pre-deployment of supplies, resources and staff; changes were implemented to support this in future operations, consistent with The Stafford Act (P.L. 100-707, 1988).

Across the U.S., there will now be better future coordination of both Army National Guard and Active Duty troops while they are acting in an emergency management capacity. During Katrina they had come from mixed commands and this led to confusion and inefficiency (Hayes, 2005, n.p.).

Another item implemented after Hurricane Katrina was the development of a national coordinator for disabled Americans. This disability coordinator would provide information and operational support on how to best handle the disabled during an emergency. Further, FEMA created a program which addresses family pets. Many people historically had not gone to a shelter, because shelters did not traditionally allow them in with their animals. FEMA now has a plan for this, and this is now used nationwide across the emergency management community (FEMA, 2010).

Technology

Technological changes require emergency management to have a well-developed understanding of Information Technology (IT) systems (Reddick, 2011, 48), as well as a reserve of extra equipment. In the old days, getting a phone line up or radio antenna was the priority, nowadays, emergency management relies on network systems such as Wifi, the Internet and GIS which are generally one of the first things to go out when there's any physical damage to a building. This is especially important for city government who generally have phone services that operate over the IP network. Today, a good emergency manager working for a city will possess at least a fundamental knowledge of how servers, firewalls, ethernet cables, and the end-user hardware devices work. This of course opens up the gateway to cyber security needs, which are already an important topic for public administrators. Most of all, cost are factors in obtaining IT education and an emergency reserve of equipment which could be utilized as emergency resources during a disaster. "Lack of financial resources and support from elected officials is a perennial problem in public administration and has been identified as a barrier to the adoption of IT in emergency management" (Reddick, 2011, p.g. 58).

Conclusion

Critical changes as a result of Congressional hearings post-Katrina have led to many major policy changes, some which have been listed above. Of course, there were many smaller policy changes too, which in the future, will help with overall disaster recovery. This includes the U.S. Department of Education helping people get back to school quicker, the U.S. Department of Labor helping people get back to work quicker, and the U.S. Department of the Treasury, helping to bring cash into disaster hit locations more rapidly. Almost every single federal agency of the United States government implemented changes post-Katrina that will affect future disaster operations with a more positive outcome.

The field of emergency management has matured greatly over the last 25 years. Each disaster After-Action Report, and Lesson Learned report, contributes to that evolving of emergency management. Today, almost all cities have some sort of public administrator who either works for the city manager or for the fire department or for an emergency management bureau. Today, university education in emergency management has become quite popular, and technology is driving advancement, as is diversity which is also assisting and improving emergency management.

References

Burdeau, C., Associated Press. (2015). Katrina: 10 years under water. New York: AP Editions.

Congress. (2006, Feb. 15). A failure of initiative: Final report of the select bipartisan committee to investigate the preparation for and response to hurricane katrina. Select Bipartisan Committee. Washington, D.C. U.S. GPO. https://www.npr.org/documents/2006/feb/katrina/house_report/katrina_report_full.pdf

FEMA. (2004). National Incident Management System (NIMS). Washington, D.C.: Department of Homeland Security; Federal Emergency Management Agency.

FEMA. (2005, Oct. 25). Florida state emergency response team and FEMA continue joint response to hurricane wilma. Washington, D.C.: Department of Homeland Security; Federal Emergency Management Agency. https://www.fema.gov/vi/node/148721

FEMA. (2010). Emergency planning for household pets and service animals providing rescue, care, shelter, and essential needs. Washington, D.C.: Department of Homeland Security; Federal Emergency Management Agency. https://www.fema.gov/pdf/conferences/iaconference/2010/wednesday_830am_household_pets_intro_1.pdf

FEMA. (2016, April). The Federal Emergency management agency: Publication 1. Washington, D.C.: Department of Homeland Security; Federal Emergency Management Agency. https://www.fema.gov/media-library-data/1462196227387-c10c40e585223d22e2595001e50f1e5c/Pub1_04-07.pdf

FEMA. (2018). Implementation Guidance and Reporting. Washington, D.C.: Department of Homeland Security; Federal Emergency Management Agency. https://www.fema.gov/implementation-guidance-and-reporting

Florida Statutes. (2018). Alternate generated power capacity for motor fuel dispensing facilities. 526.143. http://www.leg.state.fl.us

GAO, (1993, Jan. 27). Disaster management: Recent Disasters Demonstrate the Need to Improve the Nation's Response Strategy. (Testimony Before the Subcommittee on VA, HUD and Independent Agencies, Committee on Appropriations, U.S. Senate.) Washington, D.C.: U.S. General Accounting Office (GAO).

Executive Order 12127, March 31, 1979

Hayes, Jr., R.J. (2015, Apr. 1). DOD Response Under the Stafford Act: A Call to Action. Joint Force Quarterly 77. National Defense University Press. http://ndupress.ndu.edu/Media/News/Article/581880/dod-response-under-the-stafford-act-a-call-to-action/

Homeland Security Act of 2002 (P.L. 107-296)

HSPD. (2003, Feb. 28). National security and homeland security presidential directive No. 5 - Signed by George Bush

Hughes, T. (2012, Feb. 2). The evolution of federal emergency response since hurricane andrew. https://www.fireengineering.com/articles/print/volume-165/issue-2/features/the-evolution-of-federal-emergency-response-since-hurricane-andrew.html

Klaene, B.J. (2016). Structural firefighting: Strategies and tactics. Burlington, MA: Jones & Bartlett Learning.

Mahin, S. A. (1998). Lessons from damage to steel buildings during the Northridge earthquake. Engineering Structures Volume 20, Issues 4–6, April–June 1998, pp. 261-270. https://doi.org/10.1016/S0141-0296(97)00032-1

O'Connor, M.C. (2017, March 30). Building codes that promote resilient design still get a mixed reception. The Journal of the American Institute of Architects. Hanley Wood Media, Inc. https://www.architectmagazine.com/practice/building-codes-that-promote-resilient-design-still-get-a-mixed-reception_o

Public Law 108-360, National Earthquake Hazards Reduction Program Reauthorization. October 25, 2004.

Public Law 100-707, The Robert T. Stafford Disaster Relief and Emergency Assistance Act. November 23, 1988.

Reddick, C. (2011). Information technology and emergency management: preparedness and planning in US states. Disasters, 35(1), 45–61. https://doi-org.ezproxy1.apus.edu/10.1111/j.1467-7717.2010.01192.x

Smith, S. (2005). Verbatim, video from FOXNEWS live at New Orleans; via https://www.youtube.com/watch?v=bCDJ3vxMHdo

White J., Whoriskey, P. (2005, Sept. 2). Planning, response are faulted. The Washington Post. http://www.washingtonpost.com/wp-dyn/content/article/2005/09/01/AR2005090102428.html

Zumbado, T. (2005). Verbatim, video from MSNBC live at New Orleans; via https://www.youtube.com/watch?v=bCDJ3vxMHdo

A Brief Examination of the Fiscal Management of International Disasters

✿ ✿ ✿

During disasters and terrorist incidents, the United States has often helped with financial, logistical and humanitarian assistance to other countries (both developed and developing countries). Yet, the U.S. is selective about who it helps, and not all international states will receive the same exact response or resources. For the most part, it is the United Nation and its cluster of sub-organizations which plays the major role in international disaster response.

Disasters affect both developed and developing countries with equal brutality. The former generally have financial restraints that developing countries do not. Further, in developing countries, building codes are generally not as robust, and inspections may not be as common and stringent as those in developed countries. In addition, developing countries often have problems with corruption, and this can manifest with structures built with less-than-quality building materials that are significantly more vulnerable to large storms, winds, earthquakes and fires. The wealth of a country is also a key aspect in their overall disaster response (Toya & Skidmore 2007; Raschky 2008). As we have seen time after time, very poor countries, such as Haiti, often face extreme consequences and an extensive road to recovery after a disaster. Zhou, Li, Wu, et al., indicate that many socio-economic factors can lead to higher casualties after a disaster, "Higher unemployment rate, lower level of education and greater gross dependency ratio could also result in the increase in [the] death toll from disasters" (p.g. 552).

A study conducted out of the University of Malaysia looked at 73 countries and concluded that "wealthy nations and their citizens are better prepared" (Padli, Muzafar & Baharom, 2010, p.g. 429) for disasters, both because of elements such as wealth and education. The latter factor has been spoken of previously by the U.N. Educational, Scientific and Cultural Organization (UNESCO), who has named education, as a key factor in reducing disaster related effects (Matsuura, 2005).

The Role of the United Nations

The United Nations has a large emergency/disaster response capability that is commonly headed under the rubric of *humanitarian response*. The UN's disaster response system can be quite complicated to the unfamiliar eye, as the system includes many organizations with related sub-agencies. This includes the *UN Office for the Coordination of Humanitarian Affairs* (OCHA) which reports to the *UN Secretariat*—one of the six major arms of the United Nations. The OCHA is the body (in coordination with various committees), which coordinates responding to worldwide emergencies (UNOCHA, 2018). Upon a disaster occurring, the OCHA may dispatch a Disaster Assessment and Coordination Team (UNDAC) to a country which has expressed the need for assistance. That team has the ability to establish an *On-Site Operations Coordination Center* (OSOCC) which is the point of contact and management team for disaster response/recovery operations.

Below OCHA is the UN *Central Emergency Response Fund* (CERF), which facilitates the most immediate and rapid initial intervention after a disaster. In 2018, the top five donors to OCHA and all of its tributaries (in order from largest to smallest dollar amount), were the United States ($50.7 M), Sweden ($37.2M), Great Britain ($35.7M), Saudi Arabia ($21.6M), and the European Commission ($16.7M), (UNOCHA, Funding, 2018).

Another division of the UN Secretariat is the *Office for Disaster Risk Reduction*, which has as its mandate, the UN *International Strategy for Disaster Reduction* (UNISDR) (Haddow, Bullock, Coppola, 2008, p.g. 256). The UNISDR serves as the "focal point in the United Nations system for the coordination of disaster reduction...." (UN, 2002). The UNISDR holds global conferences on disasters risk reduction which aim to teach political leaders about emergency management and develop policies on global disasters; it also offers grants to nations who seek to mitigate risk. The United Nations responds both to natural disasters and man-made ones. They catalogue disasters by severity, with *Level-3* (L-3) responses being the highest level of mobilization—while these can be a response to a typhoon, earthquake, famine or other natural disaster—they also can mean a response in a warzone, such as is currently going on in Syria and Yemen.

To facilitate overall management of disasters, the United Nations has developed a system which is similar in nation to the *Emergency Support Functions* of America's *National Response*

Framework. The UN system, known as the *Cluster System*, integrates how both the UN and non-UN organizations (chiefly non-governmental organizations), can best coordinate disaster response (Bissell, Jensen, & Feldman-Jensen, 2013, p.g. 344). They do this through a system in which 11 different functions / tasks which are each assigned a coordinating body. Examples include, *Nutrition* (United Nations International Children's Emergency Fund); *Emergency Telecommunications* (World Food Programme); *Protection* (United Nations High Commissioner for Refugees); *Health* (World Health Organization), etc. These UN agencies have large sophisticated sub-agencies complete with subject matter experts, authority, and the resources needed to help in a disaster.

Of course, the UN is a very large organization and has other disaster response components spread among their organization, these include the *UN Development Programme* (UNDP) and its *Disaster Reduction and Recovery Programme* (DRRP). There is also the UNDP's *Disaster Reduction Unit* (DRU) (Haddow, et al., 2008, p.g. 261). Each of the many disaster response programs and agencies all play different roles, but they all march toward the same beat, and that is to reduce the effects of disasters and reduce human suffering.

Fiscal Concerns Related to Foreign Disasters

The UN does not just respond to—but helps nations prepare for—and recover from—disasters. As previously mentioned, the OCHA offers grants for mitigation and risk reduction. Assisting the UN with global monetary issues are international financial

"The UN does not just respond to—but helps nations prepare for—and recover from—disasters."

institutions. The UN works with various global financial institutions to support disaster risk reduction and to achieve sustainable development which itself will be a factor in the creation of more resilient communities. These financial institutions are key players when it comes to insurance management of large disasters, this includes pre-disaster risk reduction, and resilience initiatives. The two largest institutions in this category are *The World Bank* (TWB) and the *International Monetary Fund* (IMF). These organizations contribute greatly to "disaster response, relief and reconstruction" (Haddow, et al., 2008, p.g. 251). These institutions help with the creation and distribution of large amounts of emergency monies, usually made up of pooled funds from several different countries:

> The purpose of a natural disaster fund is to establish a fiscal buffer to cover the potential cost of a catastrophic event in a timely manner without endangering long-term fiscal sustainability. Such funds are effective in accumulating dedicated reserves during periods that are free of catastrophic events (IMF, 2018, p.g. 7).

An example of the work of these banks in disaster relief, came in October 2018, when TWB provided $31,000,000.00 to the nation of Dominica for building more resilient community infrastructure which can stand up better to hurricanes (World Bank, 2018).

Those Who Help During Disasters

There are many international organizations that provide disaster response across the globe; this includes private and non-governmental organizations (NGOs). These are organizations such as the International Red Cross, Doctors Without Borders, World Vision, and numerous other organizations. With literally hundreds of disasters affecting the globe annually, having a cadre of private citizens of the world, organized and trained, with a clear mission, can only help in overall humanitarian relief. NGOs are made up of people which are organized for a common reason such as an expressed interest as a civic group, religious institution, or other reason where people have a willingness to help. While NGOs are individual with their own leadership, most organizations participate as a member of larger councils and joint associations made up of similar organizations (Haddow, et al., 2008, p.g. 251). Often times these NGOs have some sort of accreditation which helps validate their participation in the disaster relief efforts. For an NGO, disaster "accreditation involves an independent body that monitors compliance with a set of standards or codes and decides on accreditation accordingly" (Hilhorst, 2002).

While some of these organizations are self-funded and are private organizations, others are more formally organized and utilize mass appeal campaigns to raise both operating funds and funds for disaster relief. Still, others such as the American Red Cross have a unique place in disaster response—as the ARC is both a private non-governmental organization, but has at its core, a US Congressional charter to carry on disaster relief. While the ARC is primarily a domestic organization which conducts most of its work in the US, it has seen disaster response roles in recent international disasters and has sent specialists to assist on the ground (ARC, 2018).

References

American Red Cross. (2018). International disaster responders. https://www.redcross.org/volunteer/volunteer-opportunities/volunteer-internationally/international-disaster-responders.html

Bissell, R., Jensen, S. Feldman-Jensen, S. (Eds.) (2013). Preparedness and response for catastrophic disasters. CRC Press: Taylor & Francis Group.

Haddow, G.D., Bullock, J.A., Coppola, D.P. (2008). Introduction to emergency management (3rd ed.). Boston: Butterworth-Heinemann.

Hilhorst, D. (2002). Being good at doing good? Quality and accountability of humanitarian NGOs. Disasters, 26(3), 193–212. Retrieved from http://ezproxy.apus.edu/login?url=http://search.ebscohost.com/login.aspx?direct=true&AuthType=ip&db=mdc&AN=12227589&site=ehost-live&scope=site

IMF. (2018, June). Fiscal policy: How to manage the fiscal costs of natural disasters. International Monetary Fund. https://www.imf.org/~/media/Files/Publications/HowToNotes/howtonote1803.ashx

Matsuura, Koichiro. (2005, Jan. 3). UNESCO stands ready to extend tsunami watch system to indian ocean: Press release no. 2005-02. United Nations Educational, Scientific and Cultural Organization. http://portal.unesco.org/en/ev.php-URL_ID=24341&URL_DO=DO_TOPIC&URL_SECTION=201.html

Padli, J., Muzafar, S.H., & Baharom, A.H. (2010). Economic impact of natural disasters' fatalities. International Journal of Social Economics, 37(6), doi:http://dx.doi.org.ezproxy1.apus.edu/ 10.1108/03068291011042319

Raschky, P.A. (2008). Institutions and the losses from natural disasters. Nat Hazards Earth Syst Sci 8. doi:10.5194/nhess-8-627-2008

Toya, H., Skidmore, M. (2007). Economic development and the impacts of natural disasters. Econ Lett. 94. doi=10.1.1.660.1931

UN General Assembly (2002). Resolution 56/195. Document A/RES/56/195. http://dag.un.org/handle/11176/237766

UNOCHA (2018). About us. United Nations Office for the Coordination of
    Humanitarian Affairs https://www.unocha.org

UNOCHA (2018). Funding: OCHA donors in 2018. United Nations Office for the
    Coordination of Humanitarian Affairs https://www.unocha.org/about-
    us/funding

World Bank. (2018, Oct. 1). Press release: World bank provides us$31 million
    additional financing for disaster prevention in dominica.
    https://www.worldbank.org/en/news/press-release/2018/10/01/world-
    bank-provides-us31-million-additional-financing-for-disaster-prevention-in-
    dominica

Zhou, Y., Li, N., Wu, W., Liu, H., Wang, L., Liu, G., & Wu, J. (2014).
    Socioeconomic development and the impact of natural disasters: Some
    empirical evidences from china. Natural Hazards, 74(2), 541-554.
    doi:10.1007/s11069-014-1198-0

Contracted Emergency Management in New York

A Supplemental Resource Before, During, and After

✿ ✿ ✿

The New York State Office of General Services (OGS) has a formal multi-year contract in place with five private contracting firms to provide emergency management and homeland security services. The State conducted their due diligence and qualified these vetted awardees with a pre-negotiated agreement to provide services to agencies and municipalities across New York through a purchase order, instead of the usual formal Request for Proposal or bid—therefore expediting the obtainment of both routine and urgent services. Municipalities (both large and small) across the State may opt to use such contractors, as does New York City Emergency Management (NYCEM). The following are the firms currently contracted with the State of New York for 2019 to 2021: AshBritt, Inc., Hagerty Consulting, Inc., Phillips and Jordan, Inc., Tetra Tech, Inc., and The Olson Group, Ltd.

AshBritt, Inc., was founded in 1992. In NY, they are contracted to provide debris management, including environmental remediation, sand removal, hazardous material removal, large-scale removal of vegetative and construction debris, maritime salvage, and heavy demolition operations. AshBritt is well known to federal agencies such as FEMA and the US Army Corps for Engineers and has been a contracted responder for just about every major Stafford Act implementation since Hurricane Andrew.

Hagerty Consulting, Inc. is a national emergency management consulting firm established in 2001. It is based out of Illinois with several offices around the country. Hagerty offers services ranging from preparedness, to response and recovery. This includes mitigation support, technical data analysis, damage assessments, mass care, crisis management, incident action plan development, engineering, floodplain management, capability assessments, and everything in between. They provide consulting for every Emergency Support Function within FEMA's National Response Framework—and not only because their Executive Chairman is the former number one man from FEMA. Hagerty makes available to the State of NY highly qualified Emergency Managers, Project Managers, Grant Administrators, Subject Matter Experts, Accountants, Preparedness Analysts, Mitigation Specialists, Engineers and Scientists. Some Hagerty staff are contracted by the City of New York and work in NYCEM's Emergency Operation Center.

Phillips and Jordan, Inc., a civil heavy construction company founded in 1949, holds a state contract for removing storm deposited soil and sand, demolition, debris storage and reduction, hazardous tree removal, etc. They are contracted to work on both Private and Public property. Phillips and Jordan also perform preparedness operations such as developing Debris Management Plans.

Tetra Tech, Inc., a California-based company with 20K employees, provides consulting and engineering services; it has been around since 1966. The company supports solutions focused on water, environment, infrastructure, resource management, energy, both domestically and overseas. Being on the State contract, the City of New York has elected to utilize them for flood protection consulting, which is coordinated by NYCEM, the Mayor's Office of Resiliency, and other city agencies. Tetra Tech also provides emergency management specialists working on flood modelling and other technical analysis related to citywide hydrologic concerns. Tetra Tech is not new to New York, they have done work for other municipalities, such as developing the Multi-Hazard Mitigation Plan for the City of New Rochelle.

The Olson Group, Ltd., is a Virginia-based consulting group focusing on terrorism and preparedness. They provide planning, training, and exercise services to federal, state and local governments across the country. After Hurricane Sandy, The Olson Group provided assessments and after-action reports for NYCEM. They are contracted in NY to assist the public (pre and post disaster) with applications for federal assistance, providing applicants with hazard mitigation opportunities, providing ice and emergency meals, debris management, and a host of other disaster-related support activities.

While the New York State Department of Homeland Security and Emergency Services (FY 2019 $1.5 billion) is a robust agency, it takes more than its personnel to provide an adequate level of statewide emergency management services for upward of 20 million people. The five firms mentioned provide resources which are available, depending on an entity's budget, to support them before, during and after a disaster; these prearranged contracted firms make supplemental emergency management support services available for every municipality and State agency, for when they need it most.

The Importance of Signed Memorandums of Understanding to Mitigate Liability in the Event of a Mutual Aid Misadventure

✧ ✧ ✧

This paper focuses on the importance of local municipalities and county-level governments having signed Memorandums of Understanding (MOUs) negotiated and in place prior to a disaster, and before providing Mutual Aid (MA) to another local municipality or county. The reason for this, is to mitigate against claims and liability which may arise during an emergency incident or disaster, if someone unexpectedly gets injured or injures someone else, or their property. While there is a standardized state to state-level mutual aid compact that addresses claims and liability which may arise during a disaster, there are no standard protections for the tens of thousands of small towns, cities and counties across the country. Having signed MOUs in place which address torts and labilities are a good way to mitigate lawsuits and the potential loss of public monies.

*

There is an importance of having signed Memorandums of Understanding (MOU) in place prior to a governmental body providing mutual aid to another governmental body, during times of emergency or disaster. This is because a signed MOU can address, and therefore potentially mitigate against lawsuits which can be had against governmental bodies and subsequently endanger public monies. In the United States, there is a federal derived state-to-state legal compact which addresses potential liability issues. However, at the municipal and county level, there is no such legal agreement, leaving those governmental bodies open to potential lawsuits. A remedy to this condition, would be having an MOU in place which addresses liability.

The American tradition of helping your fellow man in need, most likely originated with the building of the country, and may have been inspired by the scriptural words of Proverbs 3:27, "Do not withhold good from the one who needs it when you have power in your hand to act" (Berlin & Brettler, 2004). Whether it was assembling to raise a new barn, or assembling for a bucket-brigade to extinguish a barn fire, communities coming together to help one another, is an age-old and time-honored tradition. As everything about American society evolved, grew larger and increasingly more formal in the 20th century, communities still came together when they needed each other, especially in times of emergency and disaster; however, the way communities grew to come together was eventually formalized, and today, that is manifest in the common use of a Memorandum of Understanding (MOU)—a common legal agreement.

An MOU details mutual concurrence on an issue or subject, between at least two, or on occasion more, parties. The MOU will identify the participating contracting parties, detail the subject matter of the agreement at hand, along with its objectives, and may discuss the main points of the agreement (Goodman, Rothstein, Hoffman, et al. Table 9-2). The MOU will be signed by both parties.

A simple example of an MOU would be one that is signed between the City of Dallas Fire Department and the City of Fort Worth Fire Department. The two municipalities are in close proximity to one another, so they instituted a signed agreement indicating they are both available to respond to one another's city during an emergency which supersedes either city's available resources or capabilities. The importance of most MOUs is that among everything they address, they also may spell out who is responsible for issues which occur during a time of assistance, such as legal liability (ASTHO, 2013 n.p.). This may include a wide range of intentional and unintentional torts, negligence, duty to act, medical malpractice, assault, battery, etc.

Memorandums of Understanding must be universally adopted to protect counties and small municipalities from liability during emergencies and disasters. There is no nation-wide policy in place that requires pre-negotiated arrangements to all parties engaging in mutual aid assistance, at the local level. Without MOUs in place, counties and municipalities put themselves in danger of lawsuits and other liabilities, and can endanger public monies.

In 1996, the Federal Emergency Management Agency (FEMA) formalized the *Emergency Management Assistance Compact* (EMAC). FEMA says this compact is "a national interstate mutual aid agreement that enables states to share resources during times of disaster" (2012, 135). EMAC is essentially a Memorandum of Understanding which "solves the problems of liability" (Bullock, Haddow, Coppola, 2018, p. 278). The vital importance of having pre-existing plans for mutual aid which include framing the idea of liabilities and other related issues is demonstrated by the words of the Director of the U.S. Government Accountability Office (GAO), Homeland Security and Justice Issues team, to Members of Congress in the report on *Actions Taken to Implement the Post-Katrina Emergency Management Reform Act of 2006*:

> FEMA has provided funds to the National Emergency Management Association (NEMA) to develop and market model intrastate mutual aid legislation. According to these officials, this model legislation provides states with a legal framework to address reimbursement, workers compensation and liability issues for official actions, and the foundation to execute mutual aid (Jenkins, Jr. 2008, p.50).

Yet, while EMAC is legally in-place across the 50 states, the District of Columbia, Puerto Rico, American Samoa, Guam, the Northern Mariana Islands, the Pacific U.S. Minor Outlying Islands, and the U.S. Virgin Islands, it does not cover America's 36,000+ municipal and township governments, nor the 3000+ counties (NLC, 2011). These near 40,000 legal public government entities are left on their own to draw up and enter into MOU's with their nearest mutual aid partners—but unfortunately this is not universally practiced.

An MOU is "important because it defines the responsibilities of each party in an agreement" (DHS, n.d. p.9). An example of how an MOU can protect a governmental body, can be seen in this scenario: What if a regional earthquake caused the need to immediately evacuate a hospital in one county to another hospital across the county line? If one hospital calls for medical assistance from a hospital in another county, who is responsible for the safety of the patients (Hodge & Anderson, 2008)? Who would be legally liable for the patients to be transported across the county line, by both private and fire department ambulances?

Lawsuits my originate from HIPAA and potential privacy information violations, to medical personnel not following their legal scope of practice, to malpractice. Further, there are both intentional and non-intentional liabilities, such what happens if a patient falls, is dropped, or expires during transport to the next county? What if in a panic, a civilian attacks a first responder and there is a physical fight with injuries, or due to traffic lights being out, there is a collision between a transporting ambulance and a car?

Another scenario: one county has a major 3 Alarm fire in the middle of the night, and requests mutual aid from a neighboring county. Together, both fire departments extinguish the fire successfully and without incident. Then, one of the ladder trucks returning back to their county is broadsided by an intoxicated vehicle operator. Perhaps this causes massive damage to the truck, and injuries to 3 firefighters. Questions that need to be asked, include: who will pay for the short and long term medical bills of the injured personnel? Will the vehicle insurance on the ladder truck cover the damages if the ladder truck was taken outside of its jurisdiction where it was insured? If it was found out after an investigation that the fire truck ran the red light on the way back—even if an intoxicated driver struck the truck, seemingly it will be the fire department to be found at fault, and this will present further questions in regard to liability.

Good government means taking actions to minimize exposure to financial liability. Having signed MOU's in place would have addressed the issues of liability in cases such as above. The MOU lays out who is responsible for what and who assumes liability for any actions of its employees and representatives—in advance and before the 3am call for mutual aid. Public monies are meant to be kept safe, and one of the methods of doing so is reducing the potential for lawsuits and claims, and if lawsuits and claims should arise, the government should demonstrate they have done all they could in advance to outline which party takes responsibility for what. The MOU prevents misunderstandings and may mitigate disputes by plainly detailing the roles and responsibilities of both parties. A robust MOU will address insurance, liability, and will be specific about which party will pay for what, and who will be the responsible party in the case of a misadventure of any sort or tort.

Relevant Background

The report: '*Emergency response: Civil liability of volunteer health professionals*,' was developed for the US Congress and issued by Vivian Chu, legislative attorney, and Congressional researcher (2011). In this paper, the author explains for Members of Congress, "the patchwork of federal and state laws" (pg. 1) which exist to cover those who volunteer during disasters, from liability claims. The author opens by telling how the 50 states and D.C., have established "varying degrees" (pg. 2) of protections for those who volunteer to be part of the mutual aid which goes from one state to another during an emergency or disaster. Certainly, all individual volunteers, as well as incorporated and unincorporated municipalities and counties, should be covered from torts and other liability claims, when in good faith sending help in the form of mutual aid. Without having pre-written and pre-negotiated Memorandums of Understanding, small government leave themselves open to unwanted legal action. The problem which needs to be examined, is that during a disaster—it's not the time to figure out the who, what, where, etc., of civil liability, protections, and negligence. "The federal and state governments enjoy sovereign immunity from suit" says Cho, and the US Supreme Court guaranteed this protect to the states in Alden v. Maine, 527 U.S. 706 (pg. 4).

The author speaks at length about the state-wide the Emergency Management Assistance Compact (EMAC), which functions as a standing MOU that includes a prearranged structure addressing legal responsibilities, tort and liability. Two weaknesses of EMAC, is that it exists only for state to state usage and that it does not "shield from liability the nonprofit or governmental entity for the actions of its volunteers" (Cho, 2011, pg.1), and this would include the full range of potential liabilities, from an innocent mistake, to gross negligence, to malicious intentional harm / damage.

In a work supported by the US Department of Health and Human Services, and published by the Institute of Medicine (National Academy of Medicine), 'Crisis Standards of Care: A Systems Framework for Catastrophic Disaster Response,' a team of MD/Ph.D.'s discuss how while hospitals and medical centers have a full-time duty to serve the ill and injured, in "anticipation of extraordinary times, such facilities have a 'duty to plan' for catastrophic incidents" (Hanfling, Altevogt, Viswanathan, & Gostin, 2012, pg. 3). Not only do they address how the federal and state governments have responsibility in planning, but the local government must as well. A large portion of this 500+ page paper, discusses developing formal universal guidelines for what they call, Crisis Standards of Care (CSC). Within the development of CSC, the paper notes the importance to address sources of liability, liability protections, and mutual aid agreements, among several other critical topics (pg. 141). It is discussed, how focusing on "liability in crisis settings" and how these issues "should be understood before an incident occurs" is important and how having clear documentation of actions (such as an MOU) "and use of standard or community guidelines can mitigate that liability" (Hanfling, et al., 2012, pg. 262). The authors provide examples on how several states, protect their volunteers—and by extension the government itself. For example, the Maryland State Torts Claims Act, "provides state personnel immunity for acts or omissions within the scope of their duties" (Table 3-2 pg. 1-64); and in Minnesota, "Volunteers during an emergency or disaster are deemed employees of the state for purposes of torts claims defense and indemnification" (Table 3-2 pg. 1-64). Several years prior to this paper put out by Hanfling et al., the Institute of Medicine released a letter report known as the 'Guidance for Establishing Crisis Standards of Care for Use in Disaster Situations' (2009). In it, they spoke positively about memorandums of understanding and mutual aid agreements, indicating these documents can help facilitate the sharing of emergency resources (pg. 48). Yet, neither the 2009, nor 2012 paper, directly address local and municipal issues relating to liability and tort protection. This includes protecting physicians who work for county or local hospitals; physicians who have claims made against them, also open up liability to the government-owned county and local hospitals.

In *'EMAC Volunteers: Liability and Workers' Compensation,'* primarily researched by Wilfredo Lopez, the, former General Counsel of the New York City Department of Health and Mental Hygiene, the well-known state to state compact was discussed. While a positive to the EMAC state-to-state compact, was that it addressed legal issues in advance of an emergency or disaster—it also presents with "gaps" (Lopez, Kershner, & Penn, 2013, pg. 1) that affect movement of aid across jurisdictions. Such a gap would include that it does not cover local government legal issues. This paper provides what could be considered good ideas, as it tells how EMAC "provides that the requesting state cover the tort liability and the responding state cover the workers' compensation liability" (Lopez, et al., 2013, pg. 1); and this can be a framework for local municipalities and counties to develop similar protections so they are not dragged into lawsuits after sharing volunteer emergency workers, equipment, or other necessary items.

Seely in *'The Home-Field Disadvantage...'* (2017), declares that we currently have a "haphazard patchwork of immunity statutes and liability standards" (pg. 899) which needs to be addressed. This *Seattle Law Review* article, covers declarations made in regard to emergencies, disasters or public health emergencies. It covers torts and immunity statutes, as well as federal law related to the same. This paper specifically focuses on physicians, who are said to be those facing the "the greatest risk of liability for the care they provide" (Seely, 2017, pg. 877). This is because "private physicians practicing in the disaster-affected state [locally] are often not granted immunity from civil liability." Therefore, "Practicing medicine during a disaster can leave a local practitioner vulnerable to many potential causes of action" (Seely, 2017, pg. 877); and, if the physician works for a local city or county hospital, like so many do, that leaves the city or county government open to claims and liability. The author outlines the types of liability a medical practitioner can be caught up in, which by extension, a city or county-owned medical facility could be potentially be presented with a liable case for. These include: negligence "under a theory of corporate negligence," "lack of due process," "criminal liability," "inadequate treatment," "Health Insurance Portability and Accountability Act (HIPAA) violations," "Americans with Disabilities Act (ADA) violations," "alleged discrimination" (Seely, 2017, pg. 877) and several other categories of complaints which can be brought up against a physician, working for a local or county hospital—in which then the hospital or government can be held liable.

In *'Regional Cooperation and Multilateral Agreements in the Provision of Public Safety,'* the authors classify and deconstruct the difference between a Restrictive Arrangement—a more binding complete document, and an Adaptive Arrangement—where the document is meant to be broad and more flexible (Andrew & Hawkins, 2012, pg. 466-477); MOUs are in this latter category. The authors utilize data from the State of Florida in analyzing "public safety agreements among municipal and county governments" (pg. 471). They report that in regard to mutual assistance, when local governments are stretched to their limit,

"...without an agreement, local governments might not be able to build the necessary capacity to cope with disasters" (Lynn, 2005 in Andrew & Hawkins, 2012, pg.471). They indicate that in regard to written agreements, including at the local level, "anticipated outputs" need to be documented, and to be successful, agreements must be backed by "...legally and economically defensible local ordinances to protect property rights (e.g., specialized equipment), protect against tort liability, and ensure the reimbursement of actual costs when performing mutual assistance" (pg.462-463). The authors hold that for an agreement to be robust, it should be backed by ordinances and laws that will protect against torts during periods of mutual assistance (pg.463).

The California Tribal Epidemiology Center issued an emergency management document expressly for cross-jurisdictional sharing, to be utilized between tribes and/or counties. This document came out of a series of interviews with members of some 80+ tribes, who were concerned with ensuring the best measures would be taken during an emergency to protect what they saw as things relevant to their tribes. They considered both natural emergencies (fires, earthquakes, volcanic eruptions, mudslides, etc.), and non-natural emergencies (terrorism, pandemics, chemical spills, bomb threats, etc.). The document promotes establishing memorandums of understanding (MOU) for mutual assistance with fellow tribes and with nearby non-tribal county governments to "define the roles and responsibilities of each party" (Wimsatt, 2017, pg. 40). Such roles generally include who is responsible for everything from workers compensation insurance, to liability for torts and other cases which may be brought up in a disaster / post-disaster scenario. Enclosed within '*Toolkit: Cross-Jurisdictional Sharing Between Tribes And Counties For Emergency Management*,' is a sample framework for an MOU between a tribe and county government, which includes Goals, Objectives, Roles, and Responsibilities as key points (pg. 46). The inclusion of the MOU framework is important in the development of my research paper, as it demonstrates the importance of promotion and development of MOUs, in a political arena in which the federal and state government do not reside—the county level, and the tribal-county level.

In '*Model Memorandum of Understanding Between Hospitals during Declared Emergencies,*' the medico-legal administration of the *Preparedness and Catastrophic Event Response* (PACER) consortium, at Johns Hopkins Center for Law and the Public's Health, examined multiple MOUs and other documents that hospitals established for use at the local level during emergencies and disasters, and found "considerable inconsistencies in their purpose, content, scope, use" (Hodge, Anderson, & Teret, 2009, pg.2), and that they didn't "reflect critical legal issues that may be implicated during declared states of emergency [or] disaster...." (pg. 2). The paper focuses on the importance of accurate MOUs which during a disaster may be put up against challenging conditions. PACER promotes a strong MOU which discuses and addresses, "Liability, Costs, and Compensation" which is put in place in advance of an emergency situation. "While exposure to liability cannot be fully eradicated, it can be significantly minimized through the clear expression of the expectations of the parties" they indicate (pg. 11).

Conclusion

Public administrators of municipalities and county governments have an inherent responsibility to protect public monies and assets. The administrative trust over the public's fiscal assets is an honor and quite a responsibility to maintain. Such maintenance includes taking measures to mitigate against the loss of public monies due to potential civil liability, torts, or claims which may occur during an emergency or disaster. The literature is filled with much about the interstate compacts which protects states against liability, but very little on the situations which play out by municipalities and county governments who are not afforded that protection.

The weakest link in this chain may perhaps be the physician and other medical providers who go to assist in another county after a disaster or emergency. Those medical professionals who work for municipal and county hospitals open up liability to the local government by being part of a municipal owned hospital. Whether the foundation of a claim was a simple innocent mistake, an error or bad choice, governments have to be ready to protect themselves from everything including unintentional negligence to malicious actions.

Public officials have public funds entrusted to them, and insomuch have a faithful obligation to protect the public treasury. Measures to do this would include establishing agreements with fellow counties and local municipalities that in the event of an emergency or disaster, they could come to another county and borrow personnel, equipment and other resources (mutual assistance). Yet, an agreement to that would not be complete, unless it laid down the responsibility of who would cover an injured employee from one county, or who would address and be responsible for torts and claims which arise out of the mutual aid event. Currently, the states have these protections written in the legislature as laws, but the municipalities and counties aren't covered.

There is a lacuna in the discussion of why it is important to have signed memorandums of understanding in place, prior to providing mutual aid during an emergency or disaster. Such MOUs will spell out and address liability coverage, worker's compensation, and how to handle any torts which may arrive. By having these in place, public monies are increasingly protected.

References

Andrew, S.A., Hawkins, C.V. (2012). Regional cooperation and multilateral agreements in the provision of public safety. The American Review of Public Administration 43(4) 460–475 DOI: 10.1177/0275074012447676

ASTHO (2013). Liability issues in emergencies. Association of State And Territorial Health Officials (ASTHO). Retrieved from astho.org/Programs/Preparedness/Public-Health-Emergency-Law/Emergency-Authority-and-Immunity-Toolkit/Liability-Issues-in-Emergencies-Fact-Sheet/

Belcher, W.L. (2009). "Editing your sentences" In writing your journal article in 12 weeks: A guide to academic publishing Success. New York, NY: Sage Publishing.

Berlin, A; Brettler, M.Z. (Eds.). (2004). The jewish study bible. Jewish Publication Society. Oxford, New York: Oxford University Press.

Bullock J., Haddow, G., Coppola, D.P. (2018). Homeland security: The essentials. Butterworth-Heinemann: Cambridge, MA.

CaseText. (2018). Y Combinator. Mountain View, CA: https://casetext.com

Claim of Anna Sofia Sjoblom. (1913). Records of district courts of the united states. Record Group 21. Anna Sofia Sjoblom vs. White Star Steamship Co.,

(Titanic). National Archives Identifier: 6210897. Washington, D.C., US National Archives and Records Administration.

Chu, V.S. (2011, January 19). Emergency response: Civil liability of volunteer health professionals. Congressional Research Service (7-5700), Washington DC.

Crocker, K. J., & Masten, S. E. (1988). Mitigating contractual hazards: Unilateral options and contract length. The RAND Journal of Economics, 19(3), 327-343. Feiock, R. C. (2007). Rational choice and regional governance.

DHS. (n.d.). Writing guide for a memorandum of understanding (MOU). U.S. Department of Homeland Security (DHS), SAFECOM. Washington DC. Retrieved from: fcc.gov/pshs/docs/clearinghouse/DHS-MemorandumOfUnderstanding.pdf

FEMA. (2012, June). Operational templates and guidance for ems mass incident deployment. Washington DC. U.S. Department of Homeland Security.

Goodman, R.A., Rothstein, M.A., Hoffman, R.E., et al. (Eds.). (2003). Law in public health practice. New York, NY: Oxford UP.

Hanfling, D., Altevogt, B.M., Viswanathan, K., Gostin, L.O. (2012, March 21). Crisis standards of care: A systems framework for catastrophic disaster response. Committee on Guidance for Establishing Crisis Standards of Care for Use in Disaster Situations; Institute of Medicine. Washington, DC. doi: 10.17226/13351

Hodge, J.G., Anderson, E., Teret, S.P., et al. (2009). Model memorandum of understanding between hospitals during declared emergencies. National Center for the Study of Preparedness & Catastrophic Event Response (PACER) Baltimore, MD: The Johns Hopkins University.

Hodge J.G., Anderson E.D. (2008). Principles and practice of legal triage during public health emergencies. New York University Annual Survey of American Law. 64(2).

Institute of Medicine. (2009). Guidance for establishing crisis standards of care for use in disaster situations: A letter report. The National Academies Press: Washington, DC. https://doi.org/10.17226/12749.

Jenkins, Jr., W.O. (2008, November 21). Actions to implement the post-katrina act: GAO-09-59R. Washington, DC: United States Government Accountability Office.

Lopez, W., Kershner, S. P., & Penn, M. S. (2013). EMAC Volunteers: Liability and Workers' Compensation. Biosecurity and Bioterrorism: Biodefense Strategy, Practice, and Science, 11(3), 217–225. http://doi.org/10.1089/bsp.2013.0040

Lynn, P. (2005). Mutual aid: Multijurisdictional partnerships for meeting regional threats. In *New realities:Law enforcement in the post 9/11 era*. Washington, DC: U.S Department of Justice, Office of Justice Programs, Bureau of Justice Assistance. Retrieved from http://www.ncjrs.gov/pdffiles1/bja/210679.pdf

NLC. (2011). Number of municipal governments & population distribution [Latest Data from 2007]. National League of Cities (NLC). Washington D.C. Retrieved from: nlc.org/number-of-municipal-governments-population-distribution

Nexis Uni. (2018). APUS Library. Charles Town, WV: American Public University System. http://ezproxy.apus.edu/login?url=https://www.nexisuni.com

PubMed. (2018). National Libraries of Medicine. Washington, DC: US Department of Health and Human Services. https://www.ncbi.nlm.nih.gov/pubmed

Seely, S. (2017, April). The home-field disadvantage: Tort liability and immunity for paid physicians during disasters within the pacific northwest emergency management arrangement member states. Seattle University Law Review: Seattle, WA.

Wimsatt, M.A. (2017). Toolkit: Cross-jurisdictional sharing between tribes and counties for emergency management. Sacramento, CA: California Tribal Epidemiology Center, California Rural Indian Health Board, Inc.

Terrorism Reshapes Emergency Management

◇ ◇ ◇

Until the late 20th century, disaster response usually meant responding to a natural disaster. However, over the years man-made disasters such as terrorist attacks have increasingly become the foci of emergency management. The attacks on the United States in 2001, were the causative event which led to the inception of the US Department of Homeland Security (DHS) and a total reorganization of America's security posture. Further, from the attacks came the passing of *The Patriot Act*, and the *National Response Framework* (NRF)—a guide which outlines how the United States Government will respond to disasters of all kinds, this includes terrorism. The NRF is a section of the US's *National Strategy for Homeland Security* (DHS, 2007). Within these documents, the new terrorist threat is not only mentioned, but is a major focus. Haddow, et al., indicate that while the Federal Emergency Management Agency's (FEMA) funding had been historically $175 million dollars (2008, p.g. 305), this dramatically changed post-2001, and in 2008, FEMA's budget request was $3.2 billion dollars, and by 2016, the FEMA budget was near $14 billion dollars (FEMA, 2017).

Terrorism has been embroidered into FEMA's comprehensive, all-hazards, risk-based approach to emergency management. This includes applying the principles of emergency management to terrorism, including mitigating, preparing, responding, and recovering from terrorism; and while the National Strategy for Homeland Security aims to disrupt and prevent terrorism in the first place, applying the principles of emergency management to terrorism seeks to reduce the overall danger of terrorism and aims to put the nation on its best footing to recover from a terrorist event if one occurs.

Looking Towards the Future

Emergency Management has come a long way since it was primary a civil defense function, evolving considerably after WWII (Haddow, et al., 2008, p.g. 386). The many different agencies which consolidated, the creation of FEMA, and several catastrophic disasters (both politically and physically catastrophic) caused emergency management in general to become stronger and more efficient, this is through policy changes as well as training and strategy improvements. Emergency managers who have traditionally ran emergency operations for city, State and the Federal government, generally have come from the military or the fire service. But as the years go by, and with the post-2001 attacks, the 'old guard' of emergency managers is being replaced with a refreshed generation. This is both good and bad, because while universities are creating new highly educated "emergency management" students, a majority of these students don't have the on the job experience, that most would say is critical to be a competent and efficient emergency manager.

Further, the emergency management sector, and its cousin, homeland security, are increasingly benefiting from both increased funding, and new technologies. Such technologies will help strengthen America's preparedness and response to disasters, and to be more efficient in the recovery measures we take post-incident. Also, the idea that FEMA now promotes that the entire community has a role to play in emergency management, is a positive. Community Emergency Response Teams, FEMA Corps, and other national disaster-related service programs have been a positive creation and only will continue to strengthen America's resilience; combine these with public-private partnerships, and the teaching of the basics of emergency management in the public school educational system (Philpott & Serluco, 2010), and the future seems bright.

References

DHS. (2007). National strategy for homeland security. US Department of Homeland Security. Washington D.C.

FEMA. (2017). Fiscal year 2017 budget. US Department of Homeland Security, FEMA. Washington D.C.

Haddow, G.D., Bullock, J.A., Coppola, D.P. (2008). Introduction to emergency management (3rd ed.). Boston: Butterworth-Heinemann.

Philpott, D., Serluco, P. (2010). Public school emergency preparedness and crisis management plan. R & L Publishers. (E-Version). http://common.books24x7.com.ezproxy1.apus.edu/toc.aspx?bookid=75465.

Trust as a Key Factor in the Public-Government Trust Dynamic for an Efficacious Response to a National Public Health Infrastructure Failure

✿ ✿ ✿

Infrastructure failures can be caused by natural events, or manmade ones. This includes the infrastructure that the healthcare and public health sectors rely on to ensure that vital healthcare and public health services are available in a national emergency. America's biodefense posture has a foundation which is based on a rapid recovery from an attack or organic outbreak. To facilitate this, citizens must comply quickly to help stabilize an unstable situation, especially ones where the public is asked to follow regulations which they may find unfavorable. The premise of this paper and its newly conducted research was to demonstrate if when citizens trust the government, government is more effective in recovering from a large-scale emergency, or when citizens are disdainful of government, citizens can impede progress. This paper combines data from both prior examples of real-world emergencies, as well as examines contemporary data from a newly conducted survey of those in emergency management and public health. It sought their opinion on the idea that when the public trusts the government, the government will be able to provide a more efficacious response and better recover from a crisis or emergency. Results from the research indicated that the dynamic between the public and the government should be nurtured, as it is seems a relationship built on trust between the public and the government may positively impact the efficaciousness of the government to respond and recover from an emergency.

Introduction

The idea of examining how the public has confidence or trust towards the government, is something social scientists have examined for more than a half a century. The question at hand is, does the functioning or failure of a relationship built on trust between the public and the government, significantly impact the efficaciousness of the government to respond and recover from an emergency? In this capacity, we mean recovering from any sort of healthcare infrastructure crisis, including an epidemic, supply chain disruption of critical medications due to a terror attack or a myriad of other causes, including a global pandemic. The thesis statement presented is when citizens trust their government, government is effective; and when citizens are disdainful of government, citizens may impede progress.

Public Trust and Government

One of the modern pioneers in the study of public trust and government is Dr. Joseph Samuel Nye Jr. who wrote extensively on the subject over past decades.[1] Nye's research and writing

---

[1] Nye is an attorney and public policy expert, that served as Dean of the Kennedy School of Government at Harvard University, and US Assistant Secretary of Defense for International Security Affairs during the Clinton administration

includes a body of literature which examines how several negative factors could sway the public's opinion of the government. This includes corruption in government (Nye, 1967); how the public believes the country is in decline (Nye, 1990); how the constitutional framework of government is favored over day-to-day operations (Nye, 1998, p. B6); and how non-governmental organizations enjoy more trust than governments (Nye, 2008). Moreover, he, along with Zelikow and King, have expounded on the idea that it is not just a domestic occurrence, but most foreign democracies are also dealing with a loss of trust towards their governments (Nye, Zelikow & King, 1997).

Back in 1964, Barnes and Gill discussed how a survey of the American public demonstrated 75% of participants believed they could trust their government, however a study conducted three decades later, showed only 15% did so (Barnes & Gill, 2000, p. 4). The authors explore the work of Derek Bok[2], who had examined quality of life changes in America from 1960 through the 1990s. Bok studied and noted that while there has been much progress over those years for Americans, including better opportunities within the realm of economics, education, the environment—and that during those years there was both a decrease in discrimination and increase in rights for women and minorities—much of the public remained without great trust of the government (Bok, 1997). As Barnes and Gill put it, "Americans [retain] a high degree of skepticism about government" (2000, p. 5).

---

[2] Bok is former Dean of Harvard Law School and former President of Harvard University.

Ultimately, there is not just one reason for the decrease in the level of trust the public has for the government. In an effort to turn around this lack of trust, many governments have enacted programs aimed at helping to build up and improve trust in their institutions. This includes many of the practices which are assembled under the rubric of the New Public Service (NPS). These practices find value in the idea of developing programs that intrinsically engage the public. Insomuch, NPS is seen as being able to make a significant difference in the dynamic between the public and the government. The Denhardt's indicate that:

> Citizen engagement, which does not rely on traditional, legally mandated participation mechanisms, and instead embraces authentic dialogue, has been shown to produce positive effects on decision making, citizenship, and governance. Citizen engagement has become increasingly importance [sic] in governance at all levels..." (Denhardt & Denhardt, 2015b, p. 667).

They continue, "If citizen engagement is done in an inauthentic manner, based on a mistrust of citizens and one-way communication, with restricted access and little follow-through, not only will it not work" (Denhardt & Denhardt, 2015a, p. 666). It seems the research has demonstrated that programs which allow the citizen to interact with the government, work best when they are not just mandated programs, but they are programs which engage the citizens from a place of intrinsic desire to have them work together on projects of mutual interest. Many municipalities and institution are still holding on and using outdated laws and regulations on public participation, and these are continuous hindrances to developing better relationships between the government and the citizenry (Leighninger, 2014).

The important relationship which has been focused on heretofore, has involved the relationship of trust between the public and the government. What will now being focused on, is how that relationship dynamic may significantly play a role in how citizen participation / compliance, can affect the government's response to a large emergency. For example, will the public accept, and will they follow, something such as a temporary order / regulation which may be instituted by emergency management officials, to help deal with a large-scale emergency, such as a public health crisis. In examining the relationship between the public and the government during an emergency, it's important to explore earlier emergency situations and examine how the public responded to those situations.

Synopsis of Present Study

The quantitative methods employed in this study consisted of data collection and analysis. Research included employing a survey—querying emergency management professionals on this topic, to obtain quantitative data that included their opinions on the concept of public trust and can it help or hinder government officials during an emergency.[3] Respondents were asked to complete an online (ad-free) survey. The format of the survey consisted of questions which ranged from "Strongly Agree" to "Strongly Disagree." The goal was to see if respondents were of a certain opinion, or if there was a trend of opinions based upon

---

[3] (See survey questions with responses in Table 1. p.43)

the survey questions. In addition to the survey, a qualitative archival review of digitized newspapers was conducted using both *ProQuest Historical Newspapers* and *Newspapers.com*. Newspapers from various metropolitan cities in the 20th century were searched, via a key word and/or key phrase search, then by reading through complete articles. This qualitative non-statistical data collected via review of archival newspapers was used to help advance foundational understanding of public willingness to comply with government orders during past national emergencies. The data was examined to provide insight and assist in theory development and was not be meant to be a source of any statistical generalization across any specific population (Corbin & Strauss, 2008; Yin, 2013).

Data Collection

Qualitative research may be collected by evaluating a multitude of original / historical materials such as ephemera, correspondence, minutes, agendas, advertisements, newspapers, etc. This study utilizes the latter, to understand the past public willingness to comply with government orders during past national emergencies. Such information collected was used to support the research question, by examining past emergencies. Utilizing digitized archives of newspapers around the United States, key word searches was used to locate news stories related to subjects such as the Spanish *Flu pandemic, SARS, Ebola*, and other key terms. Such qualitative research was conducted to obtain foundational understanding of past public responses to government orders to which they were mandated to comply with. The data was examined to provide insight and assist in theory development and was not be meant to be a source of any statistical generalization across any specific population (Corbin & Strauss, 2008; Yin, 2013). Newspaper articles were reviewed to identify past actions the government has taken, and to learn how the public either complied or didn't to those actions—such articles are a potential source of empirical data (Mills, Bonner, & Francis, 2006). Further, as it has been mentioned and examined repeatedly in the social science literature, past performance of the population can be a good indicator of future response (Ouellette & Wood, 1998; National Academies, 2007; Franklin, 2013).

On the quantitative data collection side of this study, participants were solicited / located via social media, particularly in emergency management discussion groups which consist of at least 500 or more participants; there are at least 6 of these large emergency management groups on *Linkedin*. Soliciting within the groups with a large number of members, increases the probability that a greater number of potential participants would learn about it and potentially become respondents. In a research project such as this, querying those who have worked in real-world crises and emergencies, can provide valuable insight into the research question. The survey is expected to collect at least 100-150 opinion of respondents, over a 4-week period. Respondents were asked to complete an online (ad-free) survey via the commercial survey product, *Survey Monkey*—a recognized useful tool for social science surveys (Evans, Burnett, Kendrick, et al., 2009), consisting of 7 multiple-choice questions on a seven-point Likert scale (Croasmun & Ostrom, 2011), this scale is known to be a reliable method to measure opinions, perceptions, and behaviors. The format of the survey consists of questions which range from "Strongly Agree" to "Strongly Disagree." The Likert scale was chosen because it was a good way to obtain feedback on how strongly those in emergency management feel about the research question. The questionnaire didn't consist of any correct or incorrect answers.

Past Emergencies

The influenza pandemic of 1918-1919 was caused by a highly-contagious respiratory illness known commonly as "Spanish Flu" that created a unique global public health emergency. This viral disease killed some 20-50 million people worldwide. In the United States, millions were infected, and over 675,000 perished. The pandemic not only affected civilians but caused illness and death to those who were helping to put a halt to the spread of the infection. We see fatalities from the illness affecting members of law enforcement ("Mayor," 1918); the fire service ("City hall," 1918); and medical and nursing staff ("Phoenix physician," 1918; "Need volunteer nurses," 1918; & "Masks," 1918). In order to halt the communicable disease, municipalities launched large-scale public health programs with associated regulations. Conformity to regulations safeguarded against infection, and compliance was mandated by law. Regulations included shuttering houses of worship, restaurants, theatres, dance halls and other public gathering spots. Other rules mandated quarantines, the wearing of masks, prohibitions of weddings, funerals, and even poker games. As public ire rose, monetary penalties were imposed to discourage rule-breaking. This was a harrowing period when public health came into direct conflict with public sentiment.

Official statements disseminated via newspapers to the public, were reprints of recommendations or "Authoritative

Statements." These statements often included updates on the disease affecting local or regional communities, and how people could protect themselves from it ("Flu epidemic," 1919; "Prepare against the flu," 1919). Further, these statements, issued by the US Public Health Service (PHS) on behalf of the Federal Government, updated citizens on the ongoing national campaign efforts to contain the disease ("Uncle Sam's Advice," 1918; "Dr. Royer," 1918). In one Kansas newspaper, a government-issued statement in large bold letters declared a strict quarantine must be observed. It mentioned the laws and fines which were in place, and threatened quarantine-evaders with imprisonment. "Anyone violating the above will be arrested and prosecuted" the bottom of the long article read ("A strict quarantine," 1918). A review of the newspapers 1918-1919 demonstrates that for the most part, government mandated voluntary quarantines were respected by the public. Yet, on occasion, people were prosecuted and were subsequently incarcerated for violating terms of the quarantine ("Preacher who violated," 1919).

One of the more important initial tactics to slow the spread of the virus, was the implementation and mandatory usage of cotton or gauze masks by the public. The wearing of masks was almost universally encouraged, and in many cities, it was mandated by law, "...comply with the gauze mask provision or risk immediate closing" ("Further action," 1918). There were also occasions, when the public refused to comply with a lawful order to wear a mask ("Flu mask," 1918; "46 new cases," 1918). In San Francisco, a location which had been particularly hard hit by the virus, police officers were ordered to arrest anyone caught on the street without a mask, or even wearing a mask improperly.

This was in January of 1919, and that city was suffering three dozen people dying daily, and another 500 new cases of the disease being reported every 24 hours ("Flu mask or jail," 1919). A headline from the period shouted: "CIVILIANS ATTEMPT TO EVADE THE QUARANTINE" ("Civilians," 1918).

Concurrently, as some in the public did not fully accept the wearing of the mask, there were many localities where the public did wear masks, and there were no reported issues of non-compliance. The Spanish Flu pandemic was one of several major national emergencies during the 20th century. For example, public responses and social reactions included contempt and anger toward the government immediately following the Exxon Valdez disaster and subsequent cleanup (O'Connor, 2011; Fitzpatrick, 1995). It also followed Hurricane Katrina (Young, 2006; Marlow, 2011) where disaster contingency plans didn't manifest the way they were supposed to. In the case of Katrina, this led to extended suffering of the residents who rapidly lost faith in the government. "The response to Hurricane Katrina shook the public's confidence in the ability of government at all levels to protect its citizens in a crisis" (Lieberman, 2006, n.p.). That lack of faith and trust was verbalized in many interviews which were published in the media (Krugman, 2005; Reyes, 2006) and broadcast nationwide on the evening news stations. In the summer of 2019, the Democratic Republic of the Congo (DNC) in western Africa was experiencing a significant regional epidemic of Ebola.[4] The disease continued to spread among villagers, but once the numbers got high enough and the virus was a risk of being transmitted to the population of a nearby large

---

[4] The region is strife with armed militants who fire bombed and shot and killed physicians treating Ebola patients in April of 2019.

city,[5] the World Health Organization declared the situation an international emergency (World Health Organization, 2019). Unfortunately, many of those who either were exposed to someone with Ebola or for other reasons were considered high-risk candidates to contract the disease, refused treatment as they feared the government. During this same period, reports came from the medical community detailing how locals that should be maintaining social distance and taking the threat seriously—do not, as they feel the Ebola virus either does not exist, or the government created it for control, financial gains, or other malevolent reasons (Vinck, Pham & Bindu, et al., 2019). There are also some that deny the virus is real, as *Nature* reported, "Ebola doesn't exist!" shouted a group of men in the DNC (Maxman, 2019). Social scientists from M.I.T. and Brown University, demonstrated that among Ebola affected communities, public trust in the government was "strongly positively associated with compliance" (Blair, Morse & Tsai, 2017, p. 93).

As we can see, the public having trust in the government must be viewed as a critical factor in having citizens comply with public health directives and emergency instructions during times of societal instability, public health infrastructure break-down, and crisis—because when the public distrusts the government, and doesn't comply, it can lead to an exacerbation of the situation, and can slow recovery. As Keele has said, "Without trust, leaders are unable to obtain citizen compliance without coercion" (2007, p.242).

---

[5] Goma, in the DNC, population 2 million (2019).

Findings and Conclusion

One hundred percent of valid responses to the question on respondents' opinion to the statement that *trust between the public and the government is important* are in agreement at one level or the other. 74.6% strongly agree, 23.7% agree while only 0.9% somewhat agree. Therefore, this researcher concluded that respondents are of strong positive opinion that trust between the public and the government is important. A majority of the respondents also believed that trust between the public and the government is important for sustaining a daily harmonious societal existence. A majority (95.6%) of the respondents believed that the public's trust in government is a key factor in the government providing an efficacious response to a large-scale/national emergency, only 4.4% of the respondents disagreed at one degree or the other. Further, is the respondents' opinion on the effect of the public's lack of faith or trust in the government could hinder or complicate the government's handling of a large scale/national emergency, 99.1% of the respondents agreed while only 0.9% disagree. Finally, public's positive faith and trust in the government was believed by 94.7% of the respondents that it could lead to a more efficacious response to a large-scale/national emergency by the government, while 5.3% thought otherwise.

When it comes to emergency measures and restrictions needed to be put into place during or after a large-scale/national public health emergency, the trust by the public in the government was perceived important by the majority (99.1%) of the respondents, only 0.9% disagreed.

As we have seen, trust in the government is a strong predictor of the likelihood of persons following emergency instructions, whether they will be willing to accept a vaccination, observing a quarantine, or something as simple as donning a gauze mask. Voluntary compliance of these actions by members of the public can ensure that forced compliance will not need to be implemented. Further, by extension, we can say that voluntary compliance of these measures by the public will facilitate a smoother response to a public health crisis by the government. Whether the threat is intentional bioterrorism or the unintentional importation of an infectious organism—as occurred in 2014 with Ebola—our national biodefense posture and related public health infrastructure policies hinge upon public faith in the government and their willingness to work with the authorities and to be compliant with their lawful orders.

Civic trust is critical and for the government to sincerely win over the people, they must do things which intrinsically help the population—and the population needs to see that help manifesting. When the government can't protect citizens at the basic level citizens expect, relationships are strained, and this can have implications which affect not only the short-term recovery but the long-term redevelopment efforts. For this reason, we turn now examine factors associated with public trust and the government's ability to deal with a crisis.

Public-Government Trust Dynamic

Members of society support their government by contributing to the collective pool of taxes, voting, following the rule of law, and in times of emergencies, abiding by temporary (and often unpopular) guidelines and regulations which will help contribute to the greater good of the population. Concurrently, government aims to provide a lawful and fair society, one which has the capability to properly deal with an emergency and subsequently return society to a place of equilibrium. This researcher terms this the *Public-Government Trust Dynamic*, a meaningful bond between the people and their government where both sides can profit from positive outcomes, through a symbiotic relationship which society as a whole benefits from. The Public-Government Trust Dynamic is robust when both sides accept a position where they continually seek intrinsic positive outcomes based on factors such as peace and order for society. When either of these two entities violate the dynamic, the arrangement fails, and it is to the detriment of both parties.

Key Findings and Thoughts

The analysis of the data collected demonstrates that a relationship built on trust between the public and the government can significantly impact the efficaciousness of the government to respond and recover from an emergency. Insomuch, the thesis was supported, that when citizens trust the government, the government can be more effective then when the citizens are disdainful of the government. Civic participation and trust may be increased by increasing the role members of the public can play in their community governments. Such participation should inspire further participation, and this can spread to those among the social circles of the citizen/participant (Van Berkel & Borghi, 2008). Other ideas include providing early student education on what disasters are; national response to disasters; and, informing the public on risks & threats. All of the ideas mentioned are interconnected to ultimately helping the public in general and the public health infrastructure of the nation.

While the idea of "trust" has been explored and researched in political-social context, this paper aimed to address the gap in the literature on the topic of public trust and how it relates to the efficacious of government in the management of public health emergencies, including when the public health infrastructure of the nation is damaged or otherwise interrupted. We have explained the importance of the Public-Government Trust Dynamic, a relationship which should be continually nurtured, at all levels of government. The survey within this paper has demonstrated that professional emergency management and public health respondents are of the opinion that the functioning or failure of a relationship built on trust between the public and the government, may significantly impact the efficaciousness of the government to respond and recover from an emergency. This goes along with what we have examined and demonstrated, that without trust, the citizenry may not comply with legal and sensible actions and this can lead to complications—inversely, with trust, procedures can be put in place, rules will be followed, goals can be met, and together a nation can overcome adversity in an increased efficient manner.

References

"46 new cases, 3 deaths, day's toll." (1918, Dec. 1). *The Salt Lake Tribune.*
"A strict quarantine for the influenza must be observed." (1918, Dec. 20). *The Caney Chronicle.*

Barnes, C., Gill, D. (2000). Working paper: Declining government performance? Why citizens don't trust government. State Services Commission. New Zealand. ssc.govt.nz/resources/wp9

Bok, D. (1997). "Measuring the performance of government" in Nye, S., Zelikow, P.D. & King, D.C. (1997). Why People Don't Trust Government Cambridge, Mass. Harvard University Press.

Blair, R.A., Morse, B.S. & Tsai, L.L. (2017, Jan.). Public health and public trust: Survey evidence from the Ebola Virus Disease epidemic in Liberia. *Soc Sci Med;*172:89-97. doi: 10.1016/j.socscimed.2016.11.016.

City hall: Flu cripples [fire] service. (1918, Oct. 14). *Winfield Daily Courier.*

"Civilians attempt to evade the quarantine." (1918, Oct. 22). *The Butte Miner.*

Corbin, J., & Strauss, A. (2008). Basics of qualitative research techniques and procedures for developing grounded theory. [3rd ed.] Juliet Corbin, Anselm Strauss.). Los Angeles, CA: Sage.

Croasmun, J., Ostrom, L. (2011). Using Likert-type scales in the social sciences. *Journal of Adult Education, 40*(1), 19–22.

Denhardt, J; Denhardt, R. (2015a). The new public service: Serving, not steering. Abington, UK: Routledge.

Denhardt, J., & Denhardt, R. (2015b). The new public service revisited. *Public Administration Review, 75*(5), 664–672.

"Dr. Royer Gets Support of U.S. Surgeon General." (1918, Nov. 5). *Pittsburgh Daily Post.*

Evans, R.R., Burnett, D.O., Kendrick, D.M., Et al. (2009). Developing valid and reliable online survey instruments using commercial software programs. *Journal of Consumer Health on the Internet 13*(1), 42-52.

Fitzpatrick, K. (1995). Ten guidelines for reducing legal risks in crisis management. *Public Relations Quarterly, 40*(2), 33.

"Flu epidemic will be milder." (1919, Nov. 6). *New Oxford Item.*

Franklin, K. (2013, Jan. 3). The best predictor of future behavior is...past behavior. *Psychology Today.* https://www.psychologytoday.com/us/blog/witness/201301/the-best-predictor-future-behavior-is-past-behavior

Keele, L. (2007). Social capital and the dynamics of trust in government. *American Journal of Political Science, 51*(2), 241–254. https://doi.org/10.1111/j.1540-5907.2007.00248.x

Krugman, P.P. (2005, Sep. 17). Not the New Deal. *Rutland Daily Herald.*

Leighninger, M. (2014). Want to increase trust in government? Update our public participation laws. *Public Administration Review, 74*(3), 305–306. https://doi.org/10.1111/puar.12208

Lieberman, J. (2006, Jan. 17). Senator Lieberman issues statement from Mississippi field hearing. *US Fed News Service.* Washington, DC: HT Digital Streams Limited.

Marlow, M.L. (2011). The myth of fair and efficient government: Why the government you want is not the one you get. Santa Barbara, CA: Praeger.

"Masks in Seattle." (1918, Oct. 30). *The Province.*

Mills, J., Bonner, A. & Francis, K. (2006). The development of constructivist grounded theory. *International Journal of Qualitative Methods, 5*(1), 25–35. ejournals.library.ualberta.ca/index.php/IJQM/article/view/4402/3795

"Need volunteer nurses." (1918, Oct. 16). *The Brooklyn Daily Eagle.*

Nye, J. (1967). Corruption and political development: A cost-benefit analysis. *The American Political Science Review, 61*(2), 417–427. https://doi.org/10.2307/1953254

Nye, J. (1990). Soft power. *Foreign Policy,* (80), 153-171. doi:10.2307/1148580

Nye, J.S., Zelikow, P.D., & King, D.C. (Eds.). (1997). Why people don't trust government. Cambridge, MA: Harvard University Press.

Nye, J. (2008). Public diplomacy and soft power. *The Annals of the American Academy of Political and Social Science, 616*(1), 94–109. https://doi.org/10.1177/0002716207311699

O'Connor, E. (2011). Organizational apologies: BP as a case study. *Vanderbilt Law Review, 64*(6), 1957–1991.

Ouellette, J., & Wood, W. (1998). Habit and intention in everyday life: the multiple processes by which past behavior predicts future behavior. *Psychological Bulletin, 124*(1), 54–74. https://doi.org/10.1037/0033-2909.124.1.54

"Preacher who violated flu ban sent to jail." (1919, Apr. 11). *The Tennessean.*

"Prepare against the flu, or twill be worse for you, says surgeon general blue." (1919, Sept. 14). *Pittsburgh Post-Gazette.*

"Phoenix physician dies from effects of Spanish Flu." (1918, Nov. 1). *Bisbee Daily Review.*

Reyes, B.J. (2006, Sep. 5). Coordination cited as key in crisis. *Honolulu Star-Bulletin.*

The National Academies. (2007). A strategy for assessing science: Behavioral and social research on aging. National Research Council, Division of Behavioral and Social Sciences and Education, Center for Studies of Behavior and Development, Committee on Assessing Behavioral and Social Science Research on Aging. Washington, DC: National Academies Press.

Van Berkel, R., & Borghi, V. (2008). Introduction: The governance of activation. *Social Policy and Society, 7*(3), 331–340. https://doi.org/10.1017/S1474746408004302

Vinck, P., Pham, PP.N., Bindu, K.K., et al. (2019, May 1). Institutional trust and misinformation in the response to the 2018–19 Ebola outbreak in North Kivu, DR Congo: a population-based survey. *Lancet.* Volume 19, Issue 5, P529-536

World Health Organization. (2019, Jul. 17). Ebola outbreak in the Democratic Republic of the Congo declared a public health emergency of international concern. Press Release; Geneva, Switzerland.

Yin, R.K. (1994). Case study research: Design and methods. (2nd ed.). Thousand Oaks, CA: Sage Publications.

Young, I. (2006). Katrina: Ttoo much blame, not enough responsibility. *Dissent 53*(1), 41-46. University of Pennsylvania Press. Project MUSE database.

"Uncle Sam's advice of flu." (1918, Oct. 17). *Santa Ana Register.*

Pandemic Induced Educational Changes May End 'Renaissancal Thinking' Increasing Value to All Types of Education

✿ ✿ ✿

The pandemic has been a catalyst to demonstrate a marked transformation in the American education system. It has clearly demonstrated that the traditional manner of higher education (i.e. going to university) can now be shifted online, thus forever impacting physical brick and mortal institutions. With exceptionally advancing computer technology, digitizing library stacks and making journals available online, it allows instructors and students to fulfill their academic duties from the comfort and practicality of their homes.

A university system operating a brick and mortar institution with $X as an annual budget can only accept X amount of students due to facility size and practical reasons—however, a virtual university can use that same exact $X in annual funding to hire many more instructors and open their doors to myriad more students across a vast geographic area. This is because there is no (or a decreased amount of) costs associated with physical overhead such as mortgages, faculty and support salaries, utilities, maintenance, etc.

In coming years, the idea of not (physically) "going off to college" but learning remote may help remove some of the age-old stigma from the choice of selecting to go to trade or vocational school instead of university. A trade or vocational school is a place where one can master a craft and go on to have a significantly fruitful career. As the university student may no longer have to "move away to college," this may level the social playing field across the board, if not only because both the university student and the vocational student will now be learning at home within their local community.

To help advance trade and vocational educational choices, society must get over its "Renaissancal thinking" dilemma. The Liberal Arts emerged as liberation, not anything associated with being politically liberal as we know it today. What is generally termed the Liberal Arts came about along with the birth of humanism, which was a path to human empowerment, with the pedagogic idea of the trivium and quadrivium, which were first advanced by the Romans in the 6th century. The former is language: grammar, logic, and rhetoric. The latter is numbers: arithmetic, astronomy, music, and geometry. The trivium was important as this is how humans connect with people—through words; and the quadrivium was how humans communicated with the natural world around them—via numbers. During the Renaissance, both the trivium and quadrivium were valued as fostering the unified idea of reality and "proper path" to being educated. This is not unlike how attending a university has remained what many consider the "proper path" to being educated, especially for an education which will help one lead to a good career.

"To help advance trade and vocational educational choices, society must get over its 'Renaissancal thinking' dilemma."

It was during the Renaissance that the European economy increased dramatically, as populations grew, sea trade advanced, banks developed, and increasing trade routes connecting the near-East and Asia brought about an explosion of commercial activity. Moreover, it was during this period that art and artisans diverged, and those artisans who developed their craft and both were able to (and who elected to) monetarily capitalize on it, caused their activities to be seen as illiberal arts by the classically educated of society. It was the art of formal knowledge and education that was highly valued for social status and such was obtained by mastering the trivium and quadrivium. Those members of society who lacked the trivium and quadrivium were seen as uneducated. One could say that the use of the hands over use of the brain was seen as of lesser value, and attributed to those who have mastered a lesser pure art. This was the point in history which one can see the separation of "art" and "artisans," or—those who predominantly work through the mastery of language and science versus those who are considered lesser because they worked with their hands.

Today, the artisan continues to work with their hands to create both beautiful and functional technologically artistic creations, such as engines, micro-computers and machinery in various forms—all of these which are expressive creations, as are writing literature, painting, composing music, or solving equations. Yet, it is the continued antiquated Renaissancal thinking which continues to stifle the flowering of the modern technological artisans and their trades, maintaining that it is only university education and not vocational and technical education which have intrinsic value in our modern society.

The young people of today need to be encouraged, and not taught (either directly or indirectly), that trade and vocations are some sort of "illiberal art" which they should avoid as a choice for their life's work. Maybe now as university education undergoes a sea change due as a result of the pandemic, we shall see an increased merit of trade and vocational educational, and perhaps society will see all education as intrinsically good no matter where or how or how it is obtained.

Disaster-Oriented Public Private Partnerships

✿ ✿ ✿

T here are many different ways that the government, federal, state, city, may legally interact with the private sector. This may include entering into contractual agreements, developing memorandums of understanding, or entering into an entity which is existed for over a century—that being the Public Private Partnership. These are contractual agreements between a government agency and a private-sector organizations such as a corporation. An early example of this can be found in 19th century America, during the active railroad construction boom. The principle was that a private sector entity would invest in something (such as a railroad or toll-road {as most early roads were}), then in return, the government would allow the private entity to have a monopoly on providing services, so that they could get a return on their investment (James, 1993, p.g. 710). At the same time, the government made their citizens happy, as they were now able to utilize the new road or rail system.

Public Private Partnerships

Today, a type of contractual agreement between a governmental agency and a private sector entity is known as a Public Private Partnership. Such partnerships may be short-term arrangements, but generally they're established for the long-term, and some contracts may be arranged for 20, 25 or more years. PPPs are used throughout the world, and are common in the United States. A type of PPP is Private-Sector Financing which may be used to finance exceedingly expensive but significant projects related to localized and/or state / federal infrastructure such as bridges, railways, communications, schools, waste treatment, highways, etc. (Yescombe, 2007, p.g. xv); partnerships such as these (and others) have the capability to provide solutions for a government that desires to offer services to their citizens, they help provide a way to meet the needs of the public—and these days, being proactive for the citizenry is common for those practicing modern good-government (Klijn & Teisman, 2000, p.g. 84).

Public Private Partnerships During Disasters

Significant disasters which have occurred in recent decades, have spurred the use of PPPs in the disaster management sector, especially after the attacks on our nation on September 11, 2001, and subsequent to Hurricane Katrina (Abou-bakr, 2013, p.g. 23). Abou-bakr discusses how after both of the aforementioned disasters, corporations were coming through, supplying everything from simple blankets and sundry items, to helping with the national efforts related to rescuing people and building up our nation's military arsenal. Corporations made financial donations to the government which were earmarked for the victims, and corporations shared their supply-chain expertise as well as goods, to help get truckloads of humanitarian relief on the road in rapid time to help with the national emergency (Abou-bakr, 2013). At post-Katrina hearings, Senator George Voinovich said, "I believe there is much that the Federal Government can learn from the private sector in terms of best business practices and streamlined response in the event of an emergency." Yet, Public Private Partnerships have not always been easy to implement, there may be challenges, especially when contracts, training and exercises have not been established and tested in advance; Senator Voinovich continued:

> If we expect to be successful, we will need a robust public-private partnership. I find it troubling that in some instances, private sector companies were prepared to respond swiftly to the devastation on the Gulf Coast, while the response from all levels of government were mired in bureaucracy (U.S. Congress, 2015, p.g. 22).

In regard to utilizing PPPs in a disaster, Abou-bakr notes that Uncle Sam has partnered with corporate America previously, notably during the war effort before and during WWI, but he indicates that that connection was based on a *responsive relationship* (a response to the war—a single relationship for a single event), instead of a larger more robust *strategic relationship*. The latter example he offers is the establishment of the Federal Reserve, a private entity which was created to help maintain economic stability in response to a single event (when the stock market crashed nearly 50% in 1907), but which continued operating after the 1907 incident, providing both the government and its citizens with a long-term service (Abou-bakr, 2013). The Federal Reserve system provided, and continues to provide, a benefit to the citizens of the nation—it is a demonstration of a successful PPP.

Examples of Public Private Partnerships

Other examples of productive Public Private Partnerships include New Jersey transit's popular Hudson-Bergen Light Rail system, which moves people among one of the nation's busiest commuter corridors, one that connects New Jersey suburban towns with New York City. This $2.3 billion dollar project was built on a 15-year contract relationship between the State of New Jersey and a private partner, 21st Century Rail Corporation. This joint partnership has been said to have saved 8 full years over the conventional approach to contracting / bidding / selection then building, and the joint contract between he private corporation and the State has been successfully renewed (Federal Highway Administration, Hudson, 2018).

Another example is the Denver Eagle, a regional commuter rail line system which provides 122 miles of vital urban and suburban service. This project was developed between the City of Denver and a group of private corporations, and a financial services company. This PPP was unique as it was the first "...Commuter rail in the U.S. to include design-build, financing, and long-term operations" (Federal Highway Administration, Eagle, 2018).

While a PPP can be cooperative, they're not always symbiotic in a typical sense. While some PPPs will help both parties. It's not unusual for the government to seek a PPP where the private entities enters into contract with the government for no tangible benefit from the relationship. For example, in 1996, the U.S. Public Health Service and the Federal Emergency Management Agency sought and located a partner in the

University of Colorado Medical Center. The federal government was looking for a partner to help provide logistical and office space support for a nascent National Disaster Medical System response team. The University was happy to help, and saw the request as a way to contribute towards their civic responsibility; other than bragging rights and a simple press release, they did not earn any funding or other fiscal reward. At the same time, the two federal agencies were supported with no-cost office and warehouse space for the *National Response Team for Weapons of Mass Destruction*, a place for their team to hold meetings, and for operational coordination. Years later, the PPP stands, and the relationship has evolved and remains healthy (Alfassa, S. Personal Communications from the Office of Assistant Secretary of Health under U. S. Surgeon General, RADM Audrey F. Manley's administration, Email, 1997).

While PPPs presented above were examples of success, there are challenges faced in the development and implementation of these agreements. From negotiations and complexity of contracts, to divergent interests of stakeholders and qualifications of parties involved, the development of a PPP can be complex and a tedious progression.

Conclusion

Public Private Partnerships have a role to play between America's government and the private sector. As mentioned, a PPP can be used during a disaster, such as the response to Katrina. However, PPPs can also find a role to play before a disaster occurs, such as in the case of natural hazard mitigation—or man-made, such as mitigating a terrorist's attempt to injure or destroy our nation's critical infrastructure. The companies that own real estate in New York City are an example of how when partnered with (city) government, they have created safe pedestrian areas and explosive stand-off zones using defensive architecture, in an event to mitigate the impact of a potential future terrorist attack. The city government provides the subject-matter experts and technological assistance, and the private companies build the areas on their property (generally around buildings) using partial city funds. Also, in New York City, the Police Department has a PPP known as 'NYPD Shield' which provides training, unclassified but strategic information, and addresses concerns of the public sector. For all of these reasons, it seems Public Private Partnerships will have a future in emergency management.

References

Abou-bakr, A.J. (2013). Managing disasters through public-private partnerships. Washington, DC: Georgetown University Press.

Federal Highway Administration. (2018). Project Profile: Hudson-Bergen Light Rail. U.S. Department of Transportation. Federal Highway Administration. Washington, D.C. https://www.fhwa.dot.gov/ipd/project_profiles/nj_hudson_bergen.aspx

Federal Highway Administration. (2018). Project Profile: Eagle Project. U.S. Department of Transportation. Federal Highway Administration. Washington, D.C. https://www.fhwa.dot.gov/ipd/project_profiles/co_eagle_project.aspx

James, J.A. (1993, Sept.). *Changes in economic instability in 19th-century america*, American Economic Review 83:4. Pittsburgh: American Economic Association

Klijn, E., Teisman, G.R. Governing public-private partnerships: Analysing and managing the processes and institutional characteristics of public-private partnerships. (pp. 84-103). In Osborne, S. (Ed.) (2000). Public-private partnerships theory and practice in international perspective. Abington, UK: Taylor & Francis.

U.S. Congress. (2005, Nov. 16). Hurricane katrina: What can the Government learn from the private Sector's response? Hearing before the committee on homeland security and governmental affairs, united states senate. (109th Congress, 1st Session). Committee on Homeland Security and Governmental Affairs. Washington, D.C., Government Printing Office.

Yescombe, E.R. (2007). Public-private partnerships: Principles of policy and finance. Amsterdam, Netherlands: Elsevier.

NYC Drops its Guard Against Hostile Vehicle Attacks

Restaurant Patrons Risk Injury and Death as the City and Restaurant Owners are Opened up to Massive Potential Liability

✧ ✧ ✧

People are congregating, businesses are reopening, and outdoor seating seems to be the way New York City restaurants have compromised to make this happen. Yet, these temporary measures have introduced a profoundly serious risk that must be considered—that of pedestrians being at risk of being struck by an intentional or unintentional vehicle.

The 'Hostile Vehicle Attack' has been a standard offensive tactic of terrorists for the past several years. This attack is easy to pull off, instils a heavy footprint of fear in those who witness it or hear about it, and it is effectively lethal. Such attacks have happened at street fairs, bus stops, restaurants, holiday markets and other locations. The standard to protect pedestrians is the use of high-strength crash-rated steel bollards. Bollards are so important for modern perimeter security that a New York City Councilman introduced legislation to protect pedestrians waiting in the city's 10,000 bus stops with steel bollards. Those bus stops are on the sidewalk—but now, due to COVID social distancing, NYC is allowing citizens to eat outside both on the sidewalk and in the streets at unprotected restaurant tables.

Over the last few years, ramming attacks have been ever-increasing. Some of the notable incidents include a man who drove a van through the streets of Barcelona killing 13 and injuring 130. In Melbourne a driver deliberately crashed his car into a group of pedestrians on a sidewalk injuring over a dozen. In North Carolina a man drove a car into a restaurant killing people. In New York City a man drove a car at a high rate of speed across sidewalks in Times Square injuring 20 and ending the life of 1 person. Then, several months later, a man driving a truck murdered 8 people by driving on a Manhattan pedestrian and bicycle path.

> *"NYC is allowing citizens to eat outside both on the sidewalk and in the streets at unprotected restaurant tables."*

The two latter events were a catalyst for New York City to harden areas where the public was vulnerable to attack from a hostile vehicle. Since those NYC attacks, the city has spent between $50-$70 million dollars on hardening targets such as popular pedestrian plazas and certain streets using steel perimeter security bollards. Today, everything has changed as a result of the COVID Pandemic, and now NYC is allowing restaurants which had been shuttered for months, to open, and serve food to people who are sitting at tables and chairs on busy sidewalks and streets.

Steel anti-ram bollards keep vehicles at bay, no matter the intent of the driver. They halt vehicles from entering prohibited areas, their purpose is to protect pedestrians, property, and structures. NYC addresses such vulnerabilities through their 'Security Infrastructure Working Group' which is comprised of the Mayor's Office, New York Police Department, Department of Transportation, and several other participating agencies. However, since the recent reopening of the businesses, NYC has seemly dropped all concern for public safety and has allowed restaurants to place pedestrians in the streets with no physical protection—not even the 'protection' of the 6-inch sidewalk curb.

The U.S. Department of Homeland Security has warned about attacks against pedestrians, indicating terrorist groups will likely continue to encourage "unsophisticated tactics such as vehicle-ramming" since these types of attacks are difficult to prevent and "could inflict mass casualties if successful." Those same eyes on America's streets—eyes of the adversary, are still out there. If a bad actor wanted to strike and hurt innocent Americans, there would be nothing to stop them. It is important that cities which are reopening, even in staggered stages, be cognizant of where they put the public, both figuratively and literally.

NYC abides by the New York State 'Interim Guidance for Outdoor and Take-Out/Delivery Food Services' (issued June 26, 2020). This allows restaurants to serve food to people only outside, but it is not overly specific on what "outside" means. However, New York State Executive Order No. 202.38 (issued June 6, 2020) allows for sidewalk dining, and for dining in the street if it is a "closed street." Yet, NYC has dining occurring on multiple open streets, adjacent to vehicle traffic where there is seemly no enforcement of the "closed street" rule issued by the Governor.

> *"NYC has dining occurring on multiple open streets, adjacent to vehicle traffic..."*

A municipality legally allowing business owners to seat patrons at tables in an active roadway is absorbing a massive tort risk for that government. Such potential liability should be mitigated, and fully addressed. Moreover, if a City government knows that the State prohibits an activity—and yet allows it due to ignorance or any other reason, it may be held accountable in a court of law.

At a minimum, the National Transportation Safety Board (NTSB) recommends steel barriers or bollards for all street closings where pedestrians are permitted to gather. Yet, in this case the streets are not closed, and people are seated at unprotected tables in the street.

Further, for the business owner, it is a liability of high magnitude as well as an OSHA workplace safety concern for employers—a legitimate business concern. Case law well establishes that restaurant patrons that are hurt inside or immediately around a restaurant due to a dangerous condition can legally hold the restaurant liable for injuries. One hostile vehicle into a restaurant's temporary operations in the street, can lead to numerous wrongful death and personal injury suits, medical claims, pain and suffering, etc., for all patrons; just imagine the breach of duty claim for creating a safe environment for patrons, when those patrons were placed by the restaurant to dine in the street in unprotected seating areas.

In the event of an injurious incident, the catalyst won't matter if it was an intentional attack, or perhaps an infirm person who has an unexpected medical episode behind the wheel. The public who are currently being exposed to streets and areas where vehicles travel will be in a position to initiate litigation against all parties who placed them and/or allowed them to be there. Without a doubt, COVID restrictions and precautions have devastated the economy, and businesses need to be reopened. Still, focus should be placed on reopening along with proper risk assessment and safety considerations.

How Volunteering with the Red Cross Launched a Professional Career in Emergency Management

✿ ✿ ✿

In 1987, the year of my high school graduation, I was living in Southern California. One day, I noticed my neighbor and friend getting into his car, he was wearing a white shirt and red windbreaker which caught my eye. Curious, we spoke briefly, and that was my initial introduction to the American Red Cross (ARC). I was only 18, still unclear on life's path, so when my friend encouraged me to volunteer like he did, I decided to learn more. I visited the Orange County Chapter of the ARC, which at the time, was one of the largest and most active chapters in the country. The campus had an entire building for administration, emergency services and classrooms, and another large building where blood services and laboratories were.

Over the next year, I signed up for many classes and eventually became a responder on the local Disaster Action Team (DAT). First, with a partner and then on my own, I went to residential house fires in the middle of the night representing the Red Cross. There, I conducted ARC damage assessments and initiating casework to ensure that people had shelter, food, clothing, etc; I became a paperwork guru after just a few months, while increasing my self-confidence about the serious responsibility I had been entrusted with.

I progressed with ARC over next couple years spending many hundreds if not thousands of hours on volunteer ARC activities. I joined their First Aid Service Team (FAST), we had an ambulance and a few vans. On weekends we'd get up early and go establish medical aid stations at public events like 5 & 10K runs, helping the participants and demonstrating to the public that the American Red Cross was there to help.

In 1989 the massive Loma Prieta earthquake struck in San Francisco at 5pm. Freeways collapsed, houses shifted of their foundations, the Bay Bridge collapsed, and ultimately many tens of thousands were displaced. Along with many others from the Chapter, I was sent up north to assist. There, I helped unload trucks, set up kitchen in a public school (Marina Middle School) for mass feeding of the public. I was an Emergency Medical Technician by this point, and I joined the local Red Cross medical aid teams that were searching block by block in pick-up trucks, looking for wounded people and those who needed to be escorted back to the shelter. The ground remained shaky with aftershocks for over a week, so the Red Cross staff set up cots for sleeping under the stars on the basketball courts; this had been my first major disaster deployment, and it was all very surreal.

During the next few years, my ARC training progressed. I went on many disaster assignments, often squeezed into a hot Red Cross twelve-passenger van with others going out to the desert, mountains, or where other situations that had overwhelmed local communities. I went to the tragic Oakland Hills Firestorms in 1991 where I instructed volunteer members of the community—in impromptu classes that were set-up, on how to help the ARC which needed administrative field assistance. In Oakland, I also served as a Public Information Officer (PIO), speaking to local AM radio stations live on the air and local TV reporters. Later, I responded to the Southern California Mudslides and Big Bear Earthquakes, both major disasters for Southern California which occurred in 1992.

In 1993 I relocated to Central Florida. I was working as an EMT in a local hospital emergency room, but also volunteered at the Orlando Chapter of the ARC. I assisted in their EOC on several occasions. Including during an operation when the state was hit by the "Super Storm of the Century," a Presidentially declared disaster. These were the days before the Internet as we know it, and I established a weather command station in EOC utilizing a portable computer (8088 'Luggable' – not a laptop—they weren't invented yet) and a dial-up modem. I connected to the Internet protocol 'Gopher' which allowed me to obtain real-time weather and forecast data from the text-only hyper-linked system that existed prior to the introduction of the world wide web. I printed off important data, creating a 3-hour weather SITREP in Word Perfect on the Daisy-Wheel printer, then hung printouts on the wall, to the praise of the Red Cross EOC staff who looked at this as "the future." I always seemed to serve as a handy unofficial logistician in the EOC.

In total I donated eight years to the American Red Cross 1987-1995, serving in various capacities including volunteer first aid instructor, Disaster Action Team member, assistant to a Shelter Manager, and PIO. I also washed Red Cross vans, got filthy helping to unpack and repack storage facilities filled with supplies, helped tie down antennas and set up radio equipment.

We had BBQs, holiday parties, and I met friends, including my best friend that I had met during the Loma Prieta earthquake—who I am still very close friends with to this day. It's often not spoken of, but what you receive from volunteering with the Red Cross (or any other organization that strives to do good), is a great sense of camaraderie, esprit de corps, and fellowship.

In 2004 Florida was severely impacted by four hurricanes—Hurricane Charley, Frances, Ivan, and Jeanne, they were devastating to my community and my own home. Still, I went back and volunteered to assist with communications, serving as a Ham Radio operator (KI4GGU) in several county shelters the ARC had been coordinating.

Only at a disaster will you see a 53' tractor-trailer being unloaded by two dozen strangers, working together with all their might to provide resources for other strangers; only at a disaster will you see a handful of people—who just met—cooking together like a well-oiled machine, in a school cafeteria that had been turned into a shelter; and, only at a disaster, will you see groups come together on street corners, for an opportunity to assist, all desiring to help their community after a disaster.

Since I started volunteering as a young man with the American Red Cross some 30+ years ago, I have had a whole career. I have worked in EMS and public safety in various capacities over three decades. This includes serving as Deputy Commander and founder of a Disaster Medical Assistance Team (DMAT) and one of the CBRN national response teams for the US Public Health Service and FEMA. Today, I write emergency action plans and other mitigation, preparedness and response material for corporate America. I have a BA in Homeland Security and I'm working on an MPA in disaster management. I'm also preparing to become a Certified Emergency Manager very shortly.

I never earned a dime 'working' for the American Red Cross, but I earned a folder full of certificates for appreciation & recognition. Yet, the ARC has paid me by providing me with purpose, direction, responsibility and opportunity at a time when I was seeking a path. In my time with the ARC, I have had the pleasure of learning many life lessons and have been put into situations where I was able to interact with numerous bright, caring and talented people.

I didn't know it at the time, but my professional career in emergency management was launched the day I walked into the Red Cross office at 18 and offered to help. Insomuch, I strongly recommend young people volunteer for one of the many Red Cross programs, and for community leaders to continue to promote volunteerism across America.

Traffic Related Particulate Pollution: A Serious Occupational Hazard for Public Safety Personnel

✿ ✿ ✿

Public safety personnel that operate on busy urban highways, may be at risk from more than just traditional vehicular traffic. Although dynamic roadway, atmospheric, and population density may all play a roll—traffic-related particulate pollution is one of those "unknowns" to which police, fire and emergency medical personnel may not be aware of as a true occupational hazard.

America's urban roadways have been decaying now for decades—crumbling and rusting. If you were to examine the side of most urban roads—or look along the base of a center divider / Jersey barrier, one would see small piles of debris and dirt. Such debris is a mixture containing sand, soil, salt, silica, rubber, paint, asphalt, glass, metal shavings, broken down concrete particulates including cement, residual asbestos (from brakes, clutches and heat seals), and other displaced matter.

It's not uncommon during normal vehicle operation, that a certain measure of fuel (gasoline or diesel), oil, transmission fluid, brake fluid, and soot are released from a vehicle's undercarriage. Metals such as platinum which originate in the catalytic converters of vehicles are also expelled. Such heavy metals contribute to dangerous traffic-related particulates.[6] [7] The most common metals that emanate from burning petroleum-derived fuels, include lead, copper, cadmium, zinc, as well as the platinum group elements (PGE)—platinum, palladium, iridium, osmium, rhodium and ruthenium. Valued for specific unique properties, the latter metals are used in the electronics, medical and vehicular production industries. While all of these metals serve a constructive purpose, inadvertent inhalation of these metals and other substances, can be toxic.

The friction of tires causes roadside particulate debris to become airborne. Operating at the scene of a collision, an extrication, or other extended-period operation, puts the public safety worker in an environment where traffic-related particulate matter will be inhaled. Any major traffic accident will certainly kick up a heavy cloud of particulates, and often the dust will not resolve for some time. The spectrum of illness which may follow from inhalation may be a dust pneumonia (short term), or pulmonary cancer (many years later). The literature clearly demonstrates that traffic-related particulate matter is completely unhealthy and dangerous. An environmental study conducted in 2007, demonstrated that risks:

---

[6] See: The Cody Reeder. "Mining Platinum from the Road Part One." YouTube, 28 May 2016. 17 April 2017. youtube.com/watch?v=v5GPWJPLcHg&ab_channel=Cody%27sLab for an excellent example of such roadside debris. Also, see: "Implications of Platinum-Group Element Accumulation along U.S. Roads from Catalytic-Converter Attrition." James C. Ely, Clive R. Neal, Charles F. Kulpa, Mark A. Schneegurt, James A. Seidler, and, and Jinesh C. Jain. Environmental Science & Technology. 2001 35 (19), 3816-3822.

[7] Kana, Suk Fun; Tanner, Peter A. "Determination of platinum in roadside dust samples by dynamic reaction cell-inductively coupled plasma-mass spectrometry." Journal of Analytical Atomic Spectrometry. Issue 5, 2004.

Associated with the inhalation of platinum group elements [from] emissions from vehicle exhaust catalysts has been investigated by extracting road dust and...from the toxicological perspective, the results demonstrate potential health risks [which have] well-known toxic and allergenic effects on human beings and living organisms.[8]

Another study asserts, "Many studies on animals have confirmed the association of acute toxic effects with the metallic platinum."[9] Metals such as these are a source of health concern because not only do they accumulate in the environment, they are non-biodegradable; further, other than the occasional rain storm, highways are not cleaned, so a substantial amount of dust and debris can accumulate.

While the topic of indoor workplace exposure has had extensive toxicological research conducted on it, there is very little in regard to outdoor exposure to the same. One of the very few studies on this topic, alarmingly demonstrated a connection from roadway particulates exposure to illness, indicating, "A large population of highway workers is at risk of developing silicosis from exposure to crystalline silica."[10]

Crystalline silica, has been classified as a human lung carcinogen. Breathing in silica dust can cause silicosis, an

---

[8] Colombo C, Monhemius AJ, Plant JA. Platinum, palladium and rhodium release from vehicle exhaust catalysts and road dust exposed to simulated lung fluids. Ecotoxicol Environ Saf. 2008;71(3):722-30.

[9] Apostoli, Pietro. Elemental speciation in human health risk assessment. Geneva, World Health Organization, 2006

[10] Valiante DJ, Schill DP, Rosenman KD, Socie E. Highway repair: a new silicosis threat. Am J Public Health. 2004;94(5):876-80.

incurable and chronic fatal lung condition. The literature demonstrates that workers exposed to excessive silica may lead to them being classified as a high-risk group for respiratory diseases.[11] Silicosis has been known to the medical profession since WWII, and it remains a very serious concern to health and safety workers, so much so, the federal government has programs to mitigate against this preventable disease through the Occupational Safety and Health Administration (OSHA), the Mine Safety and Health Administration (MSHA), and the National Institute for Occupational Safety and Health (NIOSH).

Statistics from the rescue and recovery workers of 9/11, demonstrate over 5,000 cases of cancer (malignant neoplasms of the lungs, pleura, within the respiratory system, intrathoracic organs, etc.) have come about, primarily from inhalation during of the post-collapse atmosphere which included tremendous amounts of lead, asbestos, cement and drywall particulates (gypsum),[12] being in the air,[13] this also includes silica and metals.[14]

---

[11] Tavakol, E., Azari, M., Zendehdel, R., Salehpour, S., Khodakrim, S., Nikoo, S., & Saranjam, B. (2017). Risk evaluation of construction workers' exposure to silica dust and the possible lung function impairments. Tanaffos, 16(4), 295–303.

[12] Soffritti M, Falcioni L, Bua L, Tibaldi E, Manservigi M, Belpoggi F. Potential carcinogenic effects of world trade center dust after intratracheal instillation to Sprague-Dawley rats: first observation. Am J Ind Med. 2013;56(2):155-62. doi:10.1002/ajim.22109

[13] Another respiratory condition, bronchiolitis obliterans, aka World Trade Center dyspnea which is a chronic respiratory condition known to exist in those exposed at the attack site. See: Mann, J. M., Sha, K. K., Kline, G. , Breuer, F. and Miller, A. (2005), World Trade Center dyspnea: Bronchiolitis obliterans with functional improvement: A Case Report. Am. J. Ind. Med., 48: 225-229. doi:10.1002/ajim.20196

[14] Lorber, M., Gibb, H., Grant, L., Pinto, J., Pleil, J., & Cleverly, D. (2007). Assessment of inhalation exposures and potential health risks to the general population that resulted from the collapse of the World Trade Center towers.

Yet, additional dangers found in the roadside environment include fine particle-bound polycyclic aromatic hydrocarbons (PAHs) from vehicle emissions such as naphthalene, fluorine, pyrene, and a host of other noxious compounds which form during incomplete combustion of fuel.[15] These chemicals attach themselves to common roadside dirt and inhalable debris which lie on the highway surface and which can be inhaled by emergency crews working in an environment where such debris was disturbed and/or kicked up in a plume of dust.

John Hopkins Medical Center reports: "Most occupational lung diseases are caused by repeated, long-term exposure, but even a severe, single exposure to a hazardous agent can damage the lungs."[16] Even though it may take many years, exposure to traffic-related particulate pollution can cause inhalation illnesses. Consequently, it seems it would be judicious for there to be some sort of long-term study focusing on traffic-related particulate pollution and the incidence of illness among public safety workers who regularly operate on the highway.

Risk Analysis, 27(5), 1203–1221. https://doi.org/10.1111/j.1539-6924.2007.00956.x

[15] Salwa Kamal Hassan. (2018). Particle-bound polycyclic aromatic hydrocarbon in the atmosphere of heavy traffic areas in greater Cairo, Egypt: status, source, and human health risk assessment. Atmosphere, 9(10). https://doi.org/10.3390/atmos9100368

[16] "Occupational Lung Diseases." Occupational Lung Diseases. Johns Hopkins Medicine Health Library, n.d. Web. 17 Apr. 2017.

Emergency Management Nightmare: Hawaii's False Alert Crisis

✿✿✿

O n the morning of January 12, 2018, the 1.4 million residents of the State of Hawaii were shaken when cell phones on the island alerted with: "BALLISTIC MISSILE THREAT INBOUND TO HAWAII. SEEK IMMEDIATE SHELTER. THIS IS NOT A DRILL." A few seconds later a flash came across their television screens:

"...TAKE IMMEDIATE ACTION MEASURES...THIS IS NOT A DRILL."

Over the AM/FM radio came the automated spoken message:

"A MISSLE MAY IMPACT ON LAND OR SEA WITHIN MINUTES...IF YOU ARE DRIVING, PULL SAFELY TO THE SIDE OF THE ROAD AND SEEK SHELTER IN A BUILDING OR LIE ON THE FLOOR, THIS IS NOT A DRILL..."

Hawaii's emergency management / homeland security public notification system is tripartite; it consists of over 500 massive outdoor sirens, text messages to cell phones and other wireless devices, and television warnings which are sent to terrestrial broadcasters, cable television systems, wireless cable systems, satellite digital audio radio service (SDARS) providers, and direct broadcast satellite (DBS) services. This time, two of the three parts of the public notification system activated. The frightening text alert (SMS) was sent out by the Hawaii Emergency Management Agency (HI-EMA), via the FEMA Emergency Alert System (EAS), which is designed to allow the State to warn Americans within 10 minutes of authorities learning of a threat to national security or other significant emergency. While the Emergency Alert System in Hawaii is tied into a Cold War era air raid siren system, on this morning, the audible sirens never sounded.

"BALLISTIC MISSILE THREAT INBOUND TO HAWAII"

At the same time, as people in Hawaii watched the Ole Miss vs. Florida basketball game on TV, an ominous crawling red banner popped on the screen: "BALLISTIC MISSILE THREAT INBOUND TO HAWAII" put an startling fear into them. People panicked, they didn't know what to do. Some ran to their cars and sped off; there were traffic collisions as some drove through red lights and ignored traffic laws. People ran and woke others up—yet not knowing what action to take. On social media, some advised people in Hawaii should get in their bathtubs, others said they should seek ground level for shelter. Streets were filled with people running for cover, universities had students running and crying, as they ran for their lives across campus, trying to get into buildings. People horded medications and water into backpacks and ran into basements and garages. Others just sat down in the streets as if they capitulated to the menacing news and what they thought was about to occur. The public was seriously in fear.

Such a public terror was not seen in Hawaii since 1941, when an incoming air attack would become the onset of

America's entry into WWII. Today's incoming missile panic played out on social media: "I'm still shaking. My husband ran around closing windows (against radiation); I filled water containers and texted goodbye and 'I love you all' to my family." Another person wrote, "My sister in Hawaii texted me a picture of her and her kids huddled in a closet during their false alarm nuclear strike this morning..." Hawaii State Rep. Matt LoPresti told the media, that he took the warning "as serious as a heart attack" and got in the bathtub with his children, where they said "their prayers."

Nearly 40 minutes after the attack warnings, the Hawaii Emergency Management Agency confirmed that there was "no ballistic missile and that there were no computer hacks to the HI-EMA system, but it wasn't until a man went into cardiac arrest, and 911 received over 5000 calls from frantic citizens.

Ultimately, the cause of the false alarm was "human error." This is how the incident unfolded:

- 0805: A routine internal test during a shift change was initiated. This was a test that would involve the Emergency Alert System (on TV & radio), the Wireless Emergency Alert (via cell phones), but no warning sirens.
- 0807: A warning test was triggered statewide by the State Warning Point, HI-EMA.
- 0810: US Army Major General Joe Logan, the Adjutant General of the Hawaii National Guard, who is in charge of contingency plans in support of Homeland Security operations for the State of Hawaii—validated with the US Pacific Command (USPACOM) that there was no missile launch.

- 0813: The State Warning Point issued a vital cancellation that prevented the initial alert from being rebroadcast to phones that may not have received it yet. For instance, if a phone was on Airplane Mode or was turned off at 0807 when the initial alert message was dispatched.
- 0820: HI-EMA issues public notification of cancellation via social media.
- 0845: After getting authorization from FEMA, HI-EMA issued a "Civil Emergency Message" remotely over local radio and over the TV crawler banner: "False Alarm. There is no missile threat to Hawaii." They also sent a message out through SMS, via the Wireless Emergency Alert system (WEA): "False Alarm. There is no missile threat or danger to the State of Hawaii." A "Civil Emergency Message" (CEM) is a warning issued through FEMA's Emergency Alert System (EAS) to warn the public of a significant threat to public safety. Such messages are generally issued by a state authority, and are deployed by the National Weather Service. A CEM is a higher priority warning message than a Local Area Emergency (LAE), but it's less specific than a Civil Danger Warning (CDW). These alerts are defined in 47 CFR Ch.1 and Presidential Executive Order 13407 (2006) establishes that it "is the policy of the United States to have an effective, reliable, integrated, flexible, and comprehensive system to alert and warn the American people in situations of war, terrorist attack, natural disaster, or other hazards to public safety and well-being...."
- 0930: The Governor makes initial media notification.

The accidental alert of an incoming ICBM panicked over a million Americans on the islands and worried domestic and worldwide audiences over national and international news. The public remained in terrific fear for near 40 minutes. The crawling red TV alert banner stated "USPACOM has detected a missile threat to Hawaii," yet USPACOM (US Pacific Command) never detected a missile threat to Hawaii nor did USPACOM ever issue that statement. During the panic, people went into underground parking areas, seeking shelter, only to find their cell phones did not work down there. This is not the first time a Civil Danger Warning message was broadcast via human error. Just six months earlier, radio stations in Guam issued broadcasts which sparked fears of nuclear missiles being launched at that American island.

While seemingly the legal framework for how to alert the public is suitably outlined in the Code of Federal Regulations. It seems the operational side of the actual deployment of an emergency message should be reevaluated. Currently, a State asks FEMA for utilization of the EAS system, then once approved, the National Weather Service uses its communication infrastructure to deploy the message. Known as the NOAA Weather Wire Service (NWWS), the service exists to disseminate weather information, and other emergency alerts to the public. The latter is not an added job of the NWWS, but the system itself was designed to meet this mission as the national disseminator of emergency messages of all types.

Having pre-canned messages on the shelf for various potential incidents is a common accepted approach for a public affairs unit, but having a message such as what the false warning "quoted" from the US Pacific Command, may need to be reevaluated. It's understandable how Hawaii has been on edge lately due to talk of ICBM's being able to reach their state, but pre-loading potentially alarming messages into the human-controlled emergency broadcast system is like playing with a loaded gun.

The state's emergency management and homeland security officials should consider a password or other verbal command that can immediately put a cancelation into place that can be immediacy triggered in the event of another accidental incident. While many offices of emergency management generally only keep one person on the overnight shift as a watch commander / watch stander at a jurisdictional warning point, Hawaii, and other states, should consider a two-person authorization system for not only tests, but real-world emergency notifications. They need a two-person system because this can serve as a verification of an actual incident, and mitigate against a repeat false alert. Finally, there is a need for Hawaii to prepare a section in their State Multi-Hazard Mitigation Plan, their 1000 page state emergency plan—which currently has zero information on how to deal with incoming missiles or nuclear emergencies.

If nothing else, this incident has awoken civilians to the idea that an attack may be plausible, and that they should have some sort of family disaster plan. However, this human-caused incident has without doubt, tarnished many who previously would have trusted their local / state emergency authorities. It will take a reinvigorated plan of reengagement, so trust can once again be built up and the propensity of the citizenry will again trust the government.

This false alert had the potential for local, state-wide and even national negative consequences. Fortunately, the news that this was indeed a non-emergency was put into place as quickly as possible—although not soon enough. Confidently, overall the emergency management and homeland security community will see this as an exercise in mitigation against future false-alerts, and from this, America's early warning systems will be strengthened.

Uncloaked Wireless SSID As A Target Identifier Against Unique Ethnic Communities

✧ ✧ ✧

O ver the last several decades, certain groups have fallen victim to crimes and terrorism after being singled out because of their ethnicity and/or religion. The targeting of a specific group of people can be done in several different ways; one of these ways includes identifying a target population based upon their unique set of surnames. Certain populations have either "traditional" or "like" names which are chiefly found among distinct populations. Lists of these names are freely available on the Internet from sources readily available and as common as Wikipedia.

As an example, the Armenian community in America has many surnames with a suffix ending in -ian, -yan, or -jan, which are endings transliterated from the original patronymic names. And while these suffixes don't necessarily guarantee that a name is Armenian, when identified in a well-established small Armenian neighborhood such as in Glendale (Los Angeles), more than likely it's a name reflecting an Armenian family. The same can be established for other concentrated ethnic communities in America where surnames of like-originating people come from, such as the Vietnamese in "Little Saigon," Westminster, California; the Chinese of Honolulu, Hawaii; the Haitians of Miami, Florida; or the Iranians (Persians) of Los

Angeles, California (a notable population of such which are Jewish).

> *"...in our contemporary society, an offensive attack may not be physical, as much as it may be cyber-borne..."*

Speaking of Jews in America, there is a unique minority, within a minority; which exists among the large Jewish community that resides inside the borough of Brooklyn, New York. It is made up of descendants of Jews that came to America from Syria in the 20th century. The Syrian Jewish community of New York City lives among tight geographic urban borders. While there are several hundred different surnames which belong to the Syrian Jews, about 100 are most prevalent. While many of these surnames are common among all those who stem from Syria—Muslims, Christians and Jews—some are unique just to the former Jewish residents of that country.

In being alert and prepared against a physical attack, it's not unusual that in New York City, a population center with the largest Jewish community in the Western Hemisphere, to have frequent police-issued bulletins and certain days (mostly religious holidays) when vigilance is at its highest. But in our contemporary society, an offensive attack may not be physical, as much as it may be cyber-borne.

In the days immediately after the attacks of September 11, 2001, few would imagine that incredible monetary damage that would affect America and the world. According to a study by The New York Times, between physical damage, economic impact and directly related homeland security costs, the 9/11 attacks cost US tax payers some $767 billion dollars.

Wireless routers emerge from the factory with a random string of letters and numbers to identify them. This is the router's Service Set Identifier or SSID. In this case (and for unknown reasons), the purchasers choose to replace the random alpha-numeric SSID with their own family's surname. Using a smart phone application which gathers and stores SSIDs, the unique SSIDs of local home and small business network routers were collected in a section of Brooklyn, NY. These were collected from uncloaked, (aka openly-named), devices, and included in the collected data were numerous routers identified with Syrian Jewish family surnames displayed on a Google Maps overlay, with associated GPS locations.

While the availability of these surnames themselves would not typically be a vulnerability, the worldwide availability of a group of highly-identifiable unique surnames, combined with the ease of being able to obtain geographic locations associated with them on Google Maps, can certainly be exploited for unscrupulous purposes by persons with malicious intent for preoperational planning. This is concerning from a security stand point because one need not be in the local area to gather surnames or identify families; this information is openly available on the Internet and can be easily exploited by anyone across the world.

Education of the public is important to mitigate against allowing this security concern to continue. An immediate solution would be the importance of removing the family surname identifiers, and change the SSID back to a random alpha-numeric string the router originally came with. These simple steps may mitigate against any individual or community member from becoming targets of malicious actors.

Field-Deployable Resilient Temporary Networks for Special High-Profile Security Events

✿ ✿ ✿

A speciality service in the high-tech security industry that is not often discussed, is the establishment of the Resilient Temporary Network (RTN). These are temporary, field-deployable, purpose-built IP networks that can be installed and broken down quickly. Commonly, they are used by public safety and others, at events where temporary but increased situational awareness is needed. They are usually installed outdoors, often connecting buildings to mobile command post vehicles, or linking a command post in a tent to a set of high-resolution cameras, or just about any other configuration imaginable.

When the President of the United States arrives to give a speech, or when a local law enforcement agency is preparing for a major public event, the authorities always must prepare the locality for a certain level of expected criminal activity. This may be anywhere from illegal civil disobedience on the street, all the way up to preparing and anticipating a man-made act of terrorism. To meet these needs, the design and tactical implementation of a (wired or wireless), Resilient Temporary Network is employed.

On the surveillance side of the network may be numerous temporary cameras—including infrared, thermal, and night vision. The network may also include technologies such as people counters, area detection lasers, vibration sensors, etc. The Resilient Temporary Network must address all needs, such as power, uninterruptable power, or anything related to IT bandwidth, secure data services, the ability to send encrypted audio and video, etc.

"Using dynamic connections between the nodes, data packets have the availability to seek multiple paths as they travel through the network..."

While Resilient Temporary Networks can be wired (Spanning Tree Protocol {STP}) or wireless (Wireless Mesh Architecture), they essentially work in a similar manner. Yet, while each comes with a unique set of pros and cons, what both do well—is they can repair themselves. Utilizing a mesh configuration, in place of a point-to-point configuration, allows data packets to be reconfigured and re-routed around broken paths, using self-healing algorithms. Using dynamic connections between the nodes, data packets have the availability to seek multiple paths as they travel through the network, making the overall network substantially more stable. The Resilient Temporary Network must be able to maintain up-time, as mission-critical data flows across it.

The specific hardware chosen should be able to withstand changing weather conditions, and when there is trouble, must be able to recover quickly and automatically. Therefore, selection of cables, of peripherals, and of climatic conditions should be considered in advance.

As a chain is only as strong as its weakest link, information transport systems laden with associated peripherals (e.g. digital voice, data, video, sensory, imagery, etc.) are only as strong as the network they're on, and that's why these networks must be strong and resilient.

Integrating Internet Technology with Amateur Radio for Public Service Events

✿ ✿ ✿

At a Public Service event, the New York City Amateur Radio Emergency Communications Service (NYC-ARECS), a NYC based auxiliary communications service, utilized an APRS/AIS network to track the status of the world famous Staten Island Ferry for the purposes of obtaining real-time information that helped manage the flow of heavy pedestrian movement.

When not serving during a disaster, it is typical of amateur radio emergency teams throughout the United States, to provide communication support at events such as marathons, bike races and other "public service events" such as walk-a-thons. Deployment of communication team members to an event with tens of thousands of participants such as a marathon, or a bike race, provides an ideal training opportunity for radio operators to not only practice their communication and technical abilities, but to also observe and/or perform as part of the incident management system utilized by most municipalities.

This event in May of 2012, saw near a dozen radio operators stationed around the city, with one Net Control operator (Charles Hargrove, N2NOV) positioned in the Emergency Operations Center (EOC) located at Coast Guard Sector New York headquarters, located at Fort Wadsworth on Staten Island. The event was the Five Boro Bike Tour, America's largest cycling event, which consisted of over 30,000 bicyclists who rode a 40 (64-km) mile path through closed New York City highways over ten hours. The event finale included the 30,000 bicyclists riding over the Verrazano Narrows Bridge into Ft. Wadsworth, then returning to Manhattan via the Staten Island Ferry.

"...the NYC-ARECS net control operator, established a method to track the arrivals and departures of the Staten Island Ferry in the EOC..."

The large numbers of bicyclists and their bicycles created a need to monitor ferry traffic, for decision making in regard to moving large assemblies of people from the fort where they were initially gathered, to a staging area in proximity of the ferry terminal, before boarding the vessels. Utilizing data plotted on an Internet based digital map, from both the APRS (Automatic Packet Reporting System) and AIS (Automatic Identification System), the NYC-ARECS net control operator, established a method to track the arrivals and departures of the Staten Island Ferry in the EOC.

APRS is a non-voice digital communication system that was developed since the 1980s by Bob Bruninga (WB4APR), currently a senior research engineer at the United States Naval Academy. The technology has since expanded to embrace both GPS (1992) and later, the Internet. APRS can be used to transmit real-time data, short text messages, information and reports of the exact location of a person or object via a data signal sent over amateur radio frequency. It can also be used to provide weather station location, data and dates, track objects, as well as other map-related amateur radio volunteer activities including search and rescue and signal direction finding.

AIS is a vessel and shore-based transponder system that was developed by the U.S. Department of Transportation and made operational in 2002. It was originally designed for ocean going vessels that would be in compliance with the international SOLAS Convention (Safety of Life at Sea), administered by the International Maritime Organization and in the United States enforced by the U.S. Coast Guard. AIS provides continuous real-time information including a ship's identity, type, length, position, course, speed, navigational status and other safety-related information; it then takes this data and automatically makes it available to shore stations, other ships and aircraft. AIS information supplements marine radar, which continues to be the primary method of collision avoidance for water transport. AIS integrates a VHF-FM transceiver that can also combine with other electronic navigation sensors, such as GPS, gyrocompass or rate-of-turn indicator. AIS runs at 9600 bit/s (GMSK) on two marine VHF frequencies (channel 87B (161.975 MHz) or 88B (162.025 MHz), transmitting ship position reports once every 2 to 10 seconds, over an unencrypted system.

The gateway which NYC-ARECS used to maintain coordination of the ferries via both APRS and AIS data, was the popular APRS.fi website, one of the most sophisticated aggregators of RF derived mappable digital location information on the Internet.[1] APRS.fi collects data from APRS and AIS, then displays that data in a (Google sourced) real-time map. The APRS data comes through the APRS-IS (Automatic Packet Reporting System-Internet Service), the common name given to the Internet-based network which inter-connects various APRS radio networks across the earth and in space. APRS-IS is maintained and operated by volunteer amateur radio operators to provide world-wide capabilities to the amateur radio APRS RF networks and to promote the Amateur Radio service as a whole.

APRS.fi overlays and combines data from both APRS and AIS to geographically plot ships underway, as well as track them throughout their voyage, and even gather specific information about their movement.[2] This movement was tracked by the NYC-ARECS Net Control operator at the Emergency Operations Center after he used the various tools on the APRS.fi website, to manually select all the boats in the New York City Department of Transportation's (DOT) ferry fleet. Then, unique filters were employed so that only the active ferries would be tracked—as not all of the eight boats are usually in-service at any given time. Sailing between the boroughs of Manhattan and Staten Island, the Staten Island Ferry is the nation's single busiest ferry route by passenger volume. There are eight boats in the DOT fleet which travel the 5.2-mile (8.4-km) single direction run in 25 minutes. The three classes of these boats have the capacity to carry a range of passengers, some 1300, 3500 or even 6000 passengers per trip.

It is interesting to note, that the use of the APRS/AIS real-time monitoring of the boats, demonstrated, in hindsight, that a radio operator with the primary mission of reporting the location of the ferry in proximity to the Manhattan-side of the harbor—was now, no longer necessary. The observation and reporting of the geographic location of the vessels could be conducted in the EOC, but it could also be monitored and its progress reported, remotely by an offsite 'trusted agent' who is a pre-screened member of an organization's Virtual Operations Support Team (VOST).[3] While the idea of the 'VOST' is still nascent in the emergency management world, one certainly can see how the concept has potential.

While there are several websites which offer AIS tracking, APRS.fi remains ham-friendly, because along with AIS, it combines APRS (with GPS) plotting, making it a very popular site. The site is run out of Helsinki, Finland by a self-described single IT professional as a hobby, but (as he has listed on his site) "in a rather professional manner." The APRS.fi site, combined with the APRS/AIS data, allowed a New York City amateur radio emergency communications team on the other side of the world, to maintain a constant watch on their harbor boat traffic and the ferries themselves, then pass along that information to the coordinating representatives of the event, the authorities in the EOC, as well as to their own radio operators stationed on both sides of the harbor.

POSTSCRIPT:

While on that specific day NYC-ARECS did not use amateur radio operators on the boats themselves, they did utilize technology invented by amateur radio operators for amateur radio operators. The APRS-IS (Automatic Packet Reporting System-Internet Service) was started in the 1990s by Steve Dimse (K4HG) as a way to show APRS activity occurring on amateur radio frequencies to people using the World Wide Web. APRS-IS has grown into an ad-hoc network (500 servers and over 20,000 users), with a central server core that all packets pass through. Persons can access the network via amateur radio through several free amateur radio software applications, and even via their iPad or smart phone (even without a radio!)

utilizing a callsign and password to gain entry into the network which then uses the cellular phone's GPS technology.

This cellular phone APRS/GPS technology was combined with amateur radio APRS technology in June 2012 when NYC-ARECS assisted with the American Diabetes Association's annual Tour de Cure, an inter-state bicycle tour fundraiser which runs over 100 miles (160-km) from New York City into upstate New York. On that day, amateur radio operators were deployed with bicycle support crews in vehicles. Among the operators, some utilized APRS via radio and some via smart phone applications with GPS technology. All of the operators were tracked by Net Control utilizing APRS.fi so at any given moment the geographic location of the amateur radio operators (and the bicycle support crews) could be located on the 100-mile course.

Amateur radio operators that are interested in mainting their hobby and service through the use of HF/VHF/UHF radio communications, will certainly also be open to embracing new technology which can only expand the breadth and depth of the hobby. This of course may also potentially spark interest in the younger folks who already have embraced the Internet and other new digital technologies. These younger folks who may become "new hams" will be those that continue the hobby into the future and will be those who volunteer their time, equipment and skills to participate in civic-minded opportunities such as volunteering for public service events and in emergency communications.

Notes

[1] APRS.fi is one of several websites which allow you to track positions. It just happens to be the one selected for use by NYC-ARECS – which has no affiliation with the website – other than just being fans of the well-made site.

[2] It's interesting to note that as helpful as AIS is, in 2004, the Maritime Safety Committee of the International Maritime Organization (IMO) said that freely available AIS data on the Internet was "regrettable" and a threat to safety and security of vessels. Their position is to urge governments to discourage those who make available AIS data to others for publication on the Internet.

[3] Monitoring the day's activities over the VHF repeater from outside of New York City was Dennis Graiani (KC2UEW) a Certified Broadcast Technologist, who has since become an active and welcome member of NYC-ARECS.

The Evolution of American Civilian Defense into Modern Emergency Management

✧ ✧ ✧

T he Council of National Defense was an organization formed during World War I to coordinate resources and industry in support of the United States war effort.[17] It consisted of several executive cabinet secretaries as well as the heads of the Armed Services. The mission of this Council was to advise the President and heads of executive departments, on the strategic placement of industrial goods and services for potential and future use in times of war. The Council properly served its purpose during the war years, then suspended in 1921. Eighteen years later in 1939, the war in Europe awoke mayors of U.S. cities to revise plans for civilian defense.

In 1940, President Franklin D. Roosevelt established an Office for Emergency Management within the Executive Office of the President.[18] Among the tasks that office was given, was to maintain liaison between the President and the Council of National Defense, a Council that FDR revived some three days

---

[17] Created by act of Congress August 29, 1916 (39 Stat. 649; 50 U.S.C. ch.l) In 1917 when the U.S. entered the war, the Council of National Defense established a State Council Section to guide growth and work of state defense councils.
[18] Executive Order 8248 of September 8, 1939

later.[19] He had tasked the Council with coordinating the nation's defense program.[20] It was during this period that the Division of State and Local Cooperation was founded and became responsible for various emergency functions, including in 1940, local fire defense, as London-style aerial fire bombings were seen as a viable threat to U.S. soil.[21] At the time, Fiorello LaGuardia was the Mayor of New York City and the president of the U.S. *Conference on Mayors.* LaGuardia spearheaded the movement which helped get FDR to replace the Division of State and Local Cooperation with a federal office that would be more capable of helping cities and states better prepare. FDR drafted an Executive Order for an "Office of Home Defense," which soon came to fruition, but under the final name, the Office of Civilian Defense (OCD). Founded in 1941,[22] FDR gave the OCD a mandate to meet a wide array of needs, including the protection of civilian populations, the maintenance of morale, and the promotion of volunteer involvement in defense. Mayor LaGuardia eagerly became the first director of the OCD, tapped by FDR after sending the President a plan that included the development of what LaGuardia envisioned as a cabinet-level, "Vast bureaucracy that would not only engineer defense drills but deter sabotage."[23]

---

[19] Pederson, William D. (ed.) *A Companion to Franklin D. Roosevelt.* London: John Wiley & Sons, 2011.

[20] *Bulletin of the Atomic Scientists* Aug-Sep 1950. Chicago: Educational Foundation for Nuclear Science. 265

[21] Developed because the U.S. grew concerned about the threat of incendiary bombs such as those that were dropped on London, the Chemical Warfare Service of the War Department trained municipal firemen on how to deal with this threat.

[22] Executive Order 8757 May 20, 1941 (Which also created the *Civil Air Patrol.*)

[23] Goldstein, Richard. *Helluva Town: The Story of New York City During World War II.* New York: Simon and Schuster, 2010. 10

Even though it was drafted in 1941, the text of OCD's founding Executive Order is somewhat similar in scope to the mission of today's *Federal Emergency Management Agency* (FEMA). This includes the goals of the OCD that included to, "Serve as the center for the coordination of federal civilian defense [just replace *'civilian defense'* with *'emergency response'*] activities which involve relationships between the federal government and state and local governments..."[24] The OCD also established air-raid procedures, supervised black-outs, filled sandbags, and planned for protection against fire in case of attack.[25]

Civil Defense was a huge part of U.S. life during World War II. However, when the war ended, the civil defense efforts became sluggish. The OCD was abolished in 1945,[26] and between 1945 and 1949, civil defense was not given much attention.[27] However, this all changed once the Soviets tested an

---

[24] Executive Order 8757 Establishing the Office of Civilian Defense. May 20, 1941

[25] It's interesting to note that the OCD training for various civilian volunteer positions were not unlike those of the modern *Community Emergency Response Teams* (CERT), which include clearance of debris, first aid, rescue, mass feeding, traffic control, communications, etc.

[26] EO 9562, June 4, 1945 (All protective property acquired under act of January 27, 1942, and act of February 21, 1942, was transferred to Department of Commerce; liquidation of OCD fiscal affairs was assigned to Treasury Department.)

[27] But this was not a universal rule. Even during the height of the Cold War, due to indifference to publicity and planning in regard to civil defense exercises, a newspaper said that it seems, "Civil defense is a baby no one wants on his doorstep." And that same year when the president asked for a budget of $130 for civil defense, the Congress only gave $39.3. The same paper reported, "Local CD organizations all over the country are falling apart." (*The Bulletin*. July 11, 1957. Bend, OR)

atomic bomb in 1949.[28] Before the creation of the modern FEMA in 1979, the specific responsibility for civil defense in the United States was shared between a number of transitory organizations, agencies and departments.

A 1946 *War Department* study concluded that civil defense, as organized and directed by OCD, would be inadequate in any future war, and that a separate civilian agency for planning and operating civil defense matters should be set up within the War Department [which became the DoD (*Department of Defense*) the following year.[29] In 1948, the Office of Civil Defense Planning inside the DoD was founded. This agency lasted only 15 months and later closed to become the Civil Defense Liaison Office of the DoD.

Many emergency preparedness planning functions were initially vested in the National Security Resources Board (NSRB), which was established by the *National Security Act of 1947*,[30] as an independent agency to advise the President on

---

[28] "In 1949, when the Soviet Union developed its atomic bomb, America responded with an even more powerful weapon — a thermonuclear device that used a small atomic trigger to initiate a fusion reaction in hydrogen isotopes. Successfully tested in 1952, the H-bomb seemed to guarantee America's nuclear superiority. But in August 1953, the Soviets exploded their own H-bomb, and many US military experts also believed that the Soviets could deliver their new weapon via an ICBM. For the first time, the Soviets seemed poised to take the lead in the arms race." (See: *Minuteman Missile Sites: Management Alternatives, Environmental Assessment*. Legacy Resources Management Program. Department of the Interior, National Park Service, 1995. 22-26

[29] November 25, 1946 *War Department Memorandum* 400-5-5. This was the 'Bull Board,' headed by Maj. Gen. Harold R. Bull, organized to study problems of civil defense. (See: Harris, Mary U. "Significant Events in United States Civil Defense History Listed Chronologically, 1916-1974" *Information Services Office: DCPA*, Washington DC. February 7, 1975.)

[30] (61 Stat. 499), July 26, 1947

mobilization coordination. Yet, this agency was found to be ineffective, and in 1949, the NSRB's functions were transferred to the new Office of Defense Mobilization (ODM).[31] The ODM had been established to direct federal mobilization activities.[32] It absorbed functions of the Defense Production Administration,[33] to exercise general control of the defense production program. Part of ODM's duties included the ability to ensure the continuation of essential government and industry functions, particularly during times of crisis.[34] And while ODM became one of the most powerful agencies in the federal government, by 1953[35] it would go on to be consolidated with another organization, the Federal Civil Defense Administration (FCDA). Founded in 1951 by President Harry Truman, among its many missions was the distribution of posters, programs, and information about the threat of communist attacks.

In 1958, the ODM and the FCDA fully merged to form the Office of Defense and Civilian Mobilization (ODCM), with responsibility for civil defense and emergency mobilization coordination.[36] ODCM later became the Office of Civil and Defense Mobilization (OCDM), [37] whose job it was to administer the national civil defense program, and coordinate military, industrial, and civilian mobilization. In 1961, the organization's civil defense functions were transferred to the *Office of the Secretary of Defense*,[38] and the OCDM was split into the

---

[31] Reorganization Plan No. 4 of 1949, effective August 20, 1949
[32] Executive Order 10193, December 16, 1950
[33] established by Executive Order 10200, January 3, 1951
[34] aka 'Continuity of Government' (COG)
[35] Executive Order 10433
[36] Reorganization Plan No. 1 of 1958, effective July 1, 1958
[37] by an act of August 26, 1958 (72 Stat. 861)
[38] Executive Order 10952

Office of Emergency Planning (OEP)[39] and the Office of Civil Defense (OCD).[40]

OEP continued to coordinate all non-military emergency preparedness activities, principally in areas of resource utilization, civil defense, economic stabilization, post-attack rehabilitation, and government organization and continuity.[41] The organization later became the Office of Emergency Preparedness in 1968 with a mission to advise and assist the President in the coordination and determination of federal emergency preparedness policy.[42] The office was abolished with a reorganization in 1973.[43]

The OCD on the other hand had been reorganized into the DoD and administered by the *U.S. Army*,[44] coordinating military emergency preparedness activities. It continued operations until 1972 when President Richard Nixon transformed it into the Defense Civil Preparedness Agency (DCPA). The DCPA coordinated and directed federal, state, and

---

[39] by an act of September 22, 1961 (75 Stat. 630) Public Law 87-296

[40] Not to be confused with the earlier "Office of Civilian Defense" founded by FDR. (This was a JFK Executive Order, 10952 on July 20, 1961)

[41] In June 1970, the OEP released the results a study concluding that the Nation's preparedness for natural disasters was minimal to nonexistent. The Administration responded by introducing two of its most significant domestic policy changes in National Security Decision Memorandum (NSDM) 184. With this, for the first time in the history of civil defense, federal funds previously allocated for the exclusive purpose of preparing for military attacks could be shared with State and local governments for natural disaster preparedness.

[42] Executive Office of the President (EOP) by an act of October 21, 1968 (82 Stat. 1194).

[43] Reorganization Plan No. 2 of 1973, effective July 1, 1973. (In the summer of 1973, all functions of the Office of Emergency Preparedness were transferred to HUD, Treasury, and GSA.)

[44] DoD Directive 5160.50, March 31, 1964.

local civil defense program activities, including fallout shelters; chemical, biological, and radiological warfare defense; emergency communications and warning systems; post-attack assistance and damage assessment; preparedness planning; and government continuity.[45] It provided grants and offered support to states to prepare against nuclear war. It's mission included to provide preparedness assistance planning in all areas of civil defense and natural disasters. The goals of the DCPA were to provide an effective national civil defense program and planning guidance to state and local governments in their achievement of total disaster preparedness.[46] Nixon's DCPA eventually became an independent civil agency within the Pentagon, reporting to the Secretary of Defense.

Several other offices or agencies followed in the 1970's, all whom had seemingly overlapping missions and functions, this includes the Office of Preparedness of the *General Services Administration* (1973-75) and the Federal Preparedness Agency of the GSA (1975-79).[47] The early 1970's brought massive disasters

---

[45] John E. Davis, the last director of the Office of Civil Defense became the first director of the DCPA. It should be remembered that for many decades civil defense was long a responsibility of the war fighter. It was the military and their desire to keep their guard up against an enemy from encroaching on to the U.S. soil which was their main focus, not wondering what to do with a civilian population after an earthquake or hurricane struck. Davis wanted to follow the new line of thinking in the still nascent field of professional emergency management of the early 1970's, and that was to take an all-encompassing approach to hazards. Because of this, he was said to be bullish with Congress about his then forward-thinking ideas. (See: Knowles, Scott Gabriel. *The Disaster Experts: Mastering Risk in Modern America*. Philadelphia: University of Pennsylvania Press, 2011. 266)

[46] *The Virgin Islands Daily News* May 9, 1972.

[47] July 1973, as authorized by Executive Order 11725: (a) Federal Disaster Assistance Administration (FDAA) established by Secretary of Housing and Urban Development to administer natural disaster functions. (b) Office of Preparedness (OP) established by Administrator, General Services

requiring major federal response and recovery operations by the Federal Disaster Assistance Administration, established within the *Department of Housing and Urban Development* (HUD). By 1974 the *Disaster Relief Act* firmly established the process of Presidential Disaster Declarations, still, emergency and disaster support activities remained fragmented across the many bureaucracies of the federal family. Domestic nuclear catastrophe worries of the 1970's brought attention to the fact there were many parallel programs and policies existing at the state and local level, creating a sluggishness among the efficiency of federal emergency relief efforts, and compounding their complexity.

By the mid-1970's, the *National Governor's Association* was calling for a decrease in the many duplicate federal bodies that were responsible for various disaster response activities. They asked President Jimmy Carter to centralize federal emergency functions, and in 1979 (after reeling from criticism of the federal government's handling of the Three Mile Island accident),[48] the President merged the successor of the Federal Civil Defense Administration — the Defense Civil Preparedness Agency (DCPA), into a new organization, the Federal Emergency Management Agency (FEMA).[49]

Administration, to develop and coordinate civil preparedness policies and plans. (Note: Effective July 1, 1975, name changed by GSA to Federal Preparedness Agency.)

[48] Nicholson, William C. *Homeland Security Law And Policy*. Springfield: Charles C Thomas Publisher, 2005. 30

[49] Executive Order 12179 (Also see: Miskel, James F. *Disaster Response and Homeland Security: What Works, What Doesn't*. Stanford University Press, 2008. 67)

After the September 11, 2001 attacks, the concept of civil defense was revisited under the umbrella term of *homeland security* and the all-hazards approach to emergency management was once again put in the spotlight. In 2003, FEMA was merged into the Department of Homeland Security. The agency's mission as of 2012 is to support citizens and first responders to ensure that as a nation they work together to build, sustain, and improve their capability to prepare for, protect against, respond to, recover from, and mitigate all hazards.

The Hostile Vehicle Attack: An Example of Homeland Security and Emergency Management Sector Convergence

✿ ✿ ✿

P ractitioners within the Homeland Security and Emergency Management communities have seriously discussed how their respective industries converge when responding to threats and emergencies. This discussion led to an intellectual debate on determining the juncture point where the Homeland Security and Emergency Management enterprises deviate from one another. A prime reason these sectors have divided into two branches is due to the traditional employment career paths and backgrounds of those involved. This may include individuals who originated from a law enforcement background or from other public safety positions, such as the fire service.

One can surmise these discussions planted seeds that have been germinated from the oft-cited parallel role that both enterprises play in America's overall response to threats and emergencies. This is a primary reason why the number of contemporary academic programs that provide training in these similar, but different fields has increased immensely since the passing of the Homeland Security Act of 2002. A reason for having such a discussion is due to the fact that the newer generation of Emergency Managers and Homeland Security Professionals are entering into the field having earned their university degrees prior to entering the workforce. Previous generations of Emergency Managers and Homeland Security Professionals began their career paths by doing on-the-job training first and then perhaps a mid-career degree later in their career lives.

There are numerous all-hazard scenarios that require attention by both the Homeland Security and Emergency Management communities. Some examples include any large-scale terrorist attack, such as bombings, mass shootings, or Hostile Vehicles Attacks (HVA). However, some types of incidents may fall more in line with a Homeland Security situation and the same can often be said for situations that fall under the rubric of Emergency Management. This article will not visit the various all-hazard scenarios in this short piece. However, one of the clear-cut situations in which both Homeland Security and Emergency Management converge is the Hostile Vehicle Attack, or also known as the HVA.

Background

The dichotomy between the Homeland Security and Emergency Management sectors has been discussed by those within academia and in government. Today there are numerous career fields in which both the attributes of Homeland Security and Emergency Management are employed. However, this includes the standard divisions, such as mitigation, preparedness, response, and recovery in each sector.

In addition, the post 9/11 years have witnessed tremendous growth in university degrees focusing on Homeland Security, Emergency Management, or a combination of both. These courses of study often intertwine the differences of these fraternal sectors of civic duty. For example, the American Public University System (APUS) offers a BA degree in Homeland Security where classes, such as 'Emergency Planning' and 'Emergency Disaster Incident Command' are offered. Tulane University's BA in Homeland Security has courses in 'Emergency Management' and 'Health and Medical Issues in Emergency Management.' Arizona State University offers a joint BS degree in 'Emergency Management & Homeland Security.'

The co-mingling of similar topics between the various headings of Emergency Management and Homeland Security may be a bit confusing to those first entering the field. This can especially happen when topics, such as 'Emergency Planning' and 'Incident Management' are analogous to either sector. In addition, government and private agencies seeking candidates to fill jobs in Homeland Security and Emergency Management have requirements that often include desirable skills and certifications in areas, such as 'Emergency Planning' or 'Incident Management' which are equally relevant to both sectors.

History of Homeland Security and Emergency Management

It can be argued that the origins of what we call modern Homeland Security and Emergency Management originated from the US Council of National Defense (CND) which came about during World War I. The CND consisted of several executive cabinet secretaries as well as the heads of the Armed Services. The mission of this Council was to advise the President and heads of Executive departments on the strategic placement of industrial goods and services that would be needed in a national security emergency, or for use in times of war. The

Council served its purpose during the First World War and then suspended operations in 1921.

By 1940, the Council of National Defense was brought back to life as war fully erupted in Europe. U.S. mayors were increasingly concerned with the potential for having to deal with emergencies in the domestic front. At the time, President Franklin D. Roosevelt established an Office for Emergency Management within the Executive Office of the President. That office was tasked with maintaining liaison between the President and the Council of National Defense. This was a significant development in what can be considered as an early national security and incident management dichotomy that gradually evolved into both the modern Homeland Security and Emergency Management sectors.

Shared Similarities Between the Two

An important point worth mentioning is that professionals in the Homeland Security and Emergency Management sectors are those who actually prepare for emergencies; respond to emergencies, and help society recover from emergencies. Both Homeland Security and Emergency Management share commonalities, such as the training of both the National Incident Management System (NIMS) and the National Response Framework (NRF). Both NRF and NIMS are utilized by those in Homeland Security and Emergency Management—as the titles indicate at their core, "Incident Management" and "Response," that make up the essence of both sectors.

For example, the Homeland Security community offers standardized training of every federal law enforcement officer and federal agent. It also includes the mandatory study of both the National Response Framework and the National Incident Management System. The former teaches how the country is established in responding to major incidents. This includes the U.S. response doctrine, roles and responsibilities of the partner agencies which make up the NRF, and additional actions that support the national response. The latter focuses more on how agencies utilize a universal set of standards that work together to communicate and manage resources, incorporate tactics, and act collaboratively. This has been illustrated while using an interoperable approach to all-hazard incidents.

Traditionally, the mitigation, preparation, planning, and response to hurricanes, earthquakes, tornados, power failures, catastrophic fires, and other events, has been the purview of the Emergency Management community. Conversely, those in Homeland Security mitigate, prepare, plan, and respond to incidents related to high-level physical security threats. However, we see both sectors become mobilized to deal with the crisis and consequence when a certain type of emergency or terroristic event, such as a hostile vehicle attack (HVA) occurs.

The 'HVA' as a True Emergency and Security Threat

The Hostile Vehicle Attack (HVA) has become a very common method that is utilized by terrorists. This is much more common than the Vehicle Borne Improvised Explosive Device (VBIED). In fact, the use of HVA's typically occurs when a hostile actor is operating a vehicle that is meant to cause harm. The perpetrator intentionally enters a restricted or unauthorized area while driving the vehicle at a high speed in order to cause a combination of injury, death, disruption of business, or to promote a personal or group cause. Such a vehicle may be used to ram a building at high speed, a crowded pedestrian area, or it may carry an improvised explosive device. No matter the specific particulars of the attack, such an attack is of immediate joint concern to both Homeland Security and Emergency Management officials. The HVA is a true emergency and it is a true security problem to the United States.

Once a hostile vehicle makes an attack run, such as crashing a truck into an occupied hotel lobby or driving through a crowded holiday market, a full cadre of both fire and emergency services will respond to the aftermath. In a large city, such as New York, Emergency Management will respond and assist with the overall operation. They will coordinate needs, such as being the eyes and ears of the Mayor's office, coordinating the media, as well as distributing information among several agencies, such as the department of buildings, the fire department, hospitals, and NGOs such as the American Red Cross, etc.

In addition, Emergency Management will help coordinate with the immediate sheltering (if need be) of civilian casualties and will be there to assist with liaison and communications in order to obtain supplies and ensure that the necessary resources are provided for any city agency or department that may have an urgent need. Generally, Emergency Management will set up an Emergency Operation Center, where coordination of all of their activities will take place. Concurrently, the role of those who work among the Homeland Security enterprise (such as local investigators, police, federal law enforcement among others), will respond to secure a general perimeter, stop any immediate further threats, establish communications, initiate an investigation, maintain and secure the incident site to ensure evidence is minimally contaminated and such. They too will establish a Command Center where they will conduct their operations.

The roles and relationships of those who respond to a Hostile Vehicle Attack (HVA) are similar albeit different. After an HVA, the overarching goals are unified as they strive to stabilize the situation, assist the victims, obtain justice for the victims (which may mean individuals and society), and mitigate against future occurrences. Everyone's roles may be different, but they still serve a common purpose and goal. This is why it is vital for coordination and understanding of roles and functions to be streamlined and maintained in all possible scenarios.

Conclusion

Unlike a major natural disaster or any sort of stand-alone large criminal event, the HVA will call upon the resources and expertise that is found in both the Emergency Management and Homeland Security sectors. It will also call upon those who can deal with the immediate critical crisis and the subsequent consequences that will need urgent attention. While Emergency Management and Homeland Security have distinct roles, both sectors converge when dealing with this type of terrorist attack.

The intellectual debate on whether if or where there is a fine line that separates the modern Homeland Security and Emergency Management sectors will continue for quite some time. However, what is currently known is that those who have worked together as partners in each of these sectors will remain working in tandem, especially with incidents pertaining to an HVA. Those who follow each of these career paths tend to be people who often possess a mature sense of civic responsibility and a strong desire to come to the public aid when a scenario, such as an HVA causes chaos, panic, and disorder within an environment. Whenever this type of situation happens, it won't matter what hat one is wearing as long as there remains a strong culture of collaboration and coordination that is geared towards rectifying the situation.

FEMA's Policy Evolution

⚬ ⚬ ⚬

The development of the modern emergency management system in the United States has been a long time in development; the inception of America's disaster preparedness enterprise, came out of civil defense and emerged as its own sector. Several key major disasters help develop changes—everything from improved safety procedures to new laws, all with the intent of saving lives and minimizing future damage to property. It was a long and winding political and bureaucratic path to the development of the Federal Emergency Management Agency, and our federal government who is today a welcome partner in disaster preparedness and recovery with both States and local communities.

The Mississippi Flood

One of the initial roles of the federal government to better and more formally manage disasters in the 20th century, came about after the catastrophic 1927 Mississippi flood. This disaster was caused by torrential rains which caused the Mississippi river and its tributaries to peak affecting seven states. The flooding caused widespread levee failures, and some of the valleys along the river saw near 60 feet of water. Flood water remain in communities for many months, displacing large populations, with up to 700,000 people becoming homeless (Bea, 2012, p.g. 1293). The waters destroyed crops, livestock, vehicles, homes, commercial establishments, infrastructure, and caused a whopping one billion dollars in damage—"a third of the federal U.S. budget" for 1927 (Smith & Baeck, 2015, p.g. 9964).

Changes Instituted

Major changes which affected the States and the federal government were instituted after this event. The largest was the assignment of the U.S. Army Corps of Engineers (USACE) to the river flood management. The USACE development a national system of levees. Further, Congress went on to pass legislation on flood control and provided more funding for damns and other waterway management engineering.

The Dust Bowl

In 1939, the National Book Award and the Pulitzer Prize went to John Steinbeck for *The Grapes of Wrath*, his depiction of a family driven from their home by economic hardship and poor environmental conditions, due to series of droughts which contributed to the Dust Bowl in the central U.S. In the film adaption, a character laments, "Blowin' like this, year after year—blowin' the land away, blowin' the crops away, blowin' us away now" (Johnson, 1939, n.p.). While Steinbeck's account was fiction, the Dust Bowl was not. Dr. Donald Worster of University of Kansas has said that the Dust Bowl was "the worst ecological catastrophe in U.S. history (Worster in Butler, 2011, p.g. 1423, in Rubin, 2012). Excessive heat, droughts, and the associated dust storms were very real, and caused upwards of 1 billion dollars in damage and hardship for the nation—stemming from a combination of poor farming practices and less than ideal weather conditions. President Franklin Delano Roosevelt visited the stricken area, he commented, "I saw drought devastation in nine states." He remarked how "...effectively Federal and local authorities are taking care of pressing problems of relief and also how they are to work together to defend the people of this country against the effects of future droughts" (Roosevelt, 1939). The President was referring to focusing federal recovery efforts on future mitigation.

Changes Instituted

Subsequent actions after the Dust Bowl included newer adaptive farming methods and better techniques to grow crops, which contributed to flat open lands retaining more of their valuable top soil. These efforts were nothing short of what we would call today, hazard mitigation, actions which would reduce the severity of similar disasters in the future. An additional innovative practice instituted after the Dust Bowl was the recording of soil erosion measurements, something not previously done, (Hornbeck, 2012, p.g. 1502), and a new tool in measuring and mitigating future erosion.

Texas City Explosion

At 9:12am on the morning of April 16, 1947, both adult and children spectators were watching the fire department attempt to extinguish a smoldering fire on a moored ship, the *Grandcamp*, when an explosion occurred which has been hailed as the 'largest non-nuclear' explosion in the United States. This event took place at a port in Texas City in Galveston Bay, Texas. The blast and resulting fire which lasted for several days, killed over 500 people (Meyler, et al., 2007), injured over 5,000, destroyed 500 homes, several nearby ships, and resulted in thousands of automobiles and railroad cars being destroyed. The fire and explosion were related to a large volume of ammonium nitrate which was on board, and was kept in less-than-ideal conditions in flammable containers (Babrauskas, 2016). The national media gave great attention to this traumatic national event, and their focus placed attention on it to such a degree, that hearings took place in the Congress.

Changes Instituted

The Texas City explosion became a catalyst for the federal, state and local governments to play a more substantive role in the prevention response and recovery of disasters (Butler, 2012, p.g. 1261). From this event came changes I how chemicals are packaged, shipped, and prepared for prior to movement. The 1963 edition of the National Fire Protection Association's codes and standards for the handling and storage of Ammonium Nitrate "was developed and adopted in 1963, based on reports from this disaster, research, and earlier proposals" (Havel, 2008). This event had ramifications which would resonate to 1950 with the passage of major disaster legislation.

Civil Defense and the Federal Disaster Relief Act

In 1950, the U.S. passed The Federal Disaster Relief Act, which was the first legislative act to focus on comprehensive federal disaster relief. This act provided the Commander-in-Chief the Presidential authority to issue federal disaster declarations which authorized federal government agencies to issue direct assistance (financial and logistical) to both state and local authorities which were in need of assistance after a disaster. This act was "the most significant general federal disaster assistance policy adopted in the nation's history to that date" (Bea, 2012, p.g. 2000). The Federal Disaster Relief Act of 1950 was the impetus for the development of civil defense agencies across the country; this coincided with the practice of civil defense drills being conducted among organizations, government agencies and among educational establishments.

The 25-year period between 1950 and 1975 saw several different agencies and departments wearing a civil defense and/or disaster preparedness hat. A few of them, often administered by former WWII military officers, were created for military/national preparedness, but morphed into being ready for emergency response for other scenarios. That period saw agencies fail, succeed, and some of the latter would merge into several new entities.

The History and Development of FEMA

In 1958, the federal Office of Defense Mobilization (ODM) (Bea, 2012, p.g. 2033). was created to command national wartime emergency mobilization activities (E.O. 10193, 1950). It merged with the Federal Civil Defense Administration, an organization developed in 1951 by President Truman, with a focus on educating citizens on the danger of attacks by communists. Together, they would form the Office of Defense and Civilian Mobilization (ODCM), with a role of coordinating civil defense and emergency mobilizations (Reorg. Plan No. 1., 1958). The ODCM was sliced up in 1961, sending all civil defense activities to the Secretary of Defense (E.O. 10952, 1961) for coordination, and the remaining activities were cleaved into a new Office of Emergency Planning (OEP) (P.L. 87-296, 1961) and Office of Civil Defense (OCD). The Office of Emergency Planning continued to manage all emergency preparedness activities that were not related to military operations. In 1968, this office evolved into the Office of Emergency Preparedness, and its director was charged with being an advisor on matters of emergency coordination and preparedness to the President (Appropriations Act, 1968). The new OEP lasted until 1973 when it was closed, and it's duties were taken over by the departments of Housing and Urban Development, Treasury, and the General Services Administration (Reorg. Plan No. 2., 1973). Subsequently, the OCD became part of the emergency readiness program of the Department of Defense, (DoD, 1964) and stayed as a DoD asset until 1972 when President Nixon turned it into the Defense Civil Preparedness Agency (DCPA). This organization was the go-to organization for all civil defense activities at all levels of government, and was ready to assist in preparing and recovering from a man-made or natural disaster. This organization helped states prepare for atomic bomb attacks which the whole country was obsessed over at the time, even offering states grant funding. Yet, like so many or organizations, the DCPA's role would change, and it was soon after absorbed into the Pentagon, becoming an asset of the Secretary of Defense.

The 1970's

The 1970's saw a cluster of agencies and organizations with similar and sometimes overlapping missions, such as the GSA's Office of Preparedness—later—the GSA's Federal Preparedness Agency (E.O. 11725, 1973). Disasters in the 1970's which had attention focused on them, became mechanisms that created large federal responses and large federal checks being distributed to various communities, this included the HUD Federal Disaster Assistance Administration providing such assistance; no longer were federal funds only for civil defense preparedness.

Even with the 1974 *Disaster Relief Act* which steadfastly established a smooth course of action to obtain a Presidential Disaster Declaration the nation was still without a central command for disaster preparedness and response. The Three Mile Island incident and pressure by the *National Governor's Association* were part of the concluding push that would end the duplication of efforts and associated confusion of multi-agency emergency management in D.C. With the stroke of pen in 1979 (Sylves, 2012, p.g. 2563) President Jimmy Carter centralized national emergency preparedness and response, by turning the Federal Disaster Assistance Administration and the Federal Insurance Administration (both from HUD), the Defense Civil Preparedness Agency from the DoD, and the U.S. Fire Administration from the Dept. of Commerce, (Bea, 2012, p.g. 2394 & 2402), into a whole new agency, the Federal Emergency Management Agency (FEMA) (Reorg. Plan No. 3, 1978) (E.O. 12179, 1979).

Conclusion

We as a society / nation have learned lessons which will help contribute to a better system of readiness and response. Emergency management is in evolution, as an ever-growing national system for preparedness, response and recovery that has gotten better and better. The period from the early 20th century, up until the beginning of the 21ˢᵗ century, could be called the period of 'coming of age,' of the field of emergency management. The development of new operational techniques, coupled with new policy and agencies in the last several decades, no doubt has contributed to saving lives and reducing property damage—and strengthening America's overall resiliency.

References

Appropriations Act of October 21, 1968. (82 Stat. 1194)

Babrauskas, V. (2016). Explosions of ammonium nitrate fertilizer in storage or transportation are preventable accidents. Journal of Hazardous Materials. Volume 304, 5 March 2016. New York, NY: Elsevier. https://www-sciencedirect-com.ezproxy1.apus.edu/science/article/pii/S0304389415301680

Bea, K. (2012). The formative years: 1950-1978. In C. Rubin. (Ed.), *Emergency management: The American experience 1900-2010*. Boca Raton, FL: CRC Press / Taylor & Francis Group.

Butler, D. (2012). The expanding role of the federal government: 1927-1950. In C. Rubin. (Ed.), *Emergency management: The american experience 1900-2010*. Boca Raton, FL: CRC Press / Taylor & Francis Group.

DoD. (1964, March 31). Directive 5160.50

Executive Order 10193, December 16, 1950

Executive Order 10952, July 20, 1961

Executive Order 11725, July 27, 1973

Executive Order 12179, December 11, 1979

Federal Disaster Relief Act (Public Law 81-875)

Havel, G. (2008, Oct. 6). The Texas city disaster. Fire Engineering. Fairlawn, NJ: PennWell Publishing.

Hornbeck, R. (2012). The enduring impact of the American dust bowl: Short- and long-run adjustments to environmental catastrophe. American Economic

Review, 102 (4): 1477-1507.
doi:http://dx.doi.org.ezproxy2.apus.edu/10.1257/aer.102.4.1477

Johnson, N. (1939). The grapes of wrath. Screenplay; based on John Steinbeck's *The Grapes of Wrath*. (1939). New York, NY: The Viking Press-James Lloyd. http://www.dailyscript.com/scripts/grapes_of_wrath.html

Meyler, D., Stimpson, J.P., & Cutchin, M.P. (2007). Landscapes of risk: Texas city and the petrochemical industry. Organization & Environment, 20(2), 204-205,211-212.
doi:http://dx.doi.org.ezproxy2.apus.edu/10.1177/1086026607302157

Public Law 81-875, September 30, 1950 (Stat. 1109)

Public Law 87-296, September 22, 1961 (Stat. 630)

Reorganization Plan No. 1 of 1958 (5 U.S.C.)

Reorganization Plan No. 2 of 1973 (5 U.S.C.)

Reorganization Plan No. 3 of 1978 (5 U.S.C.)

Roosevelt, F.D. (1939). On the drought and the dust bowl. (national speech). Washington, D.C: The Whitehouse.
historyonthenet.com/authentichistory/1930-1939/2-fdr/3-dustbowl/ 19360906_FDR_On_The_Drought_And_The_Dust_Bowl.html

Rubin, C.B. (2012). (Ed.) Emergency management: The American experience 1900-2010 (2nd Edition for Kindle). Boca Raton, FL: CRC Press / Taylor & Francis Group.

Smith, J. A., Baeck, M.L. (2015), Prophetic vision, vivid imagination: The 1927 Mississippi river flood, *Water Resources Research*, 51, 9964–9994, doi: 10.1002/2015WR017927.

Sylves, R.T. (2012). Federal emergency management comes of age: 1979-2001. In C. Rubin. (Ed.), *Emergency management: The American experience 1900-2010*. Boca Raton, FL: CRC Press / Taylor & Francis Group.

Worster, D. (2004). Dust bowl: The southern plains in the 1930s. New York: Oxford University Press.

The Relationship of the National Response Framework, and the National Incident Management System

✧ ✧ ✧

After the attacks on America in 2001, federal authorities re-evaluated how the country responds to incidents and disasters. The first thing that was realized, is that responding and recovering from major incidents is a complex responsibility, one which requires keen attention to detail and a concurrent coordinated effort from all parts of our nation's society. This not only includes the government, but the American people as well. After only eight months of being in existence, in 2002, the newly created Department of Homeland Security issued the *National Strategy for Homeland Security* (NSHS), a 90-page framework on how to best protect the country; this guide was distributed across the nation. From this would come the subsequent National Incident Management System and the National Response Framework.

America Beef's Up Its Response Strategy

The NSHS asks for civilians to prepare themselves, and be ready to assist in their communities in the event of a nationwide incident. President W. Bush emphasized the new role of looking at disaster management by including the whole community and not just the federal government, when he said in 2002: "To best protect the American people, homeland security must be a responsibility shared across our entire Nation. As we further develop a national culture of preparedness...this strategy also calls on each of you" (NSHS, 2007, p.g. 5). More specifically, the National Strategy for Homeland Security was implemented with four specific goals, this included preventing and interrupting attacks by bad actors which seek harm against the U.S.; to ensure the protection of all U.S. citizens, U.S. resources and the country's critical infrastructure; to effectively respond to and recover from disasters and incidents of all types; and to constantly further America's resilience which will result in a more robust foundation, one which strengthen the country. From the NSHS, came a well-developed revision of the former *National Response Plan* (NRP), the *National Response Framework* (NRF). The earlier NRP had been America's plan on how to best respond to major national incidents—it, was itself an evolution of the even earlier (1992) document known as the *Federal Response Plan* (Manning & Goldfrank, 2002), p.g. 52). Yet, post-2001, with terrorism on the minds of America's law enforcement and emergency managers, the older plans were seen as being inadequate.

National Response Framework

The modern National Response Framework (NRF) is one of several guides which have been produced to offer a structure on how best respond to emergencies and disasters of all types—this now included terrorism (DHS, 2016). The NRF is a living document that is continuously revaluated. It is not only about federal response, but includes a framework for all American's to take part in overall preparedness response and recovery. As the NRF says, "This Framework is always in effect and describes the doctrine under which the Nation responds to incidents" (DHS, 2016, p.g. i).

Over the decades, and through real-world experiences, the federal government has learned that the best type of approach to a disaster is one that is scalable, and flexible; the National Response Framework is a plan such as that. It aligns the players and provides them with the responsibilities which will help best implement a response. The NRF supports the idea that the lowest governmental level, such as a city or municipality, should start the response to an incident. The multiple tiered response which the NRF emphasizes, will help initially respond to the unique needs of a local area, however once that area is overwhelmed the framework allows for the introduction of support, from upper tiers of government such as county, state or federal. The NRF integrates all disaster efforts across the five areas of emergency management which include prevention, protection, mitigation, response, and recovery.

The NRF is a foundation document that includes a listing of the Emergency Support Functions that describe federal resources typically needed in an emergency, and the agencies which oversee and would be responsible for those resources during a national incident. For example, in an emergency of national proportions, one of the most important things which is needed is continuous reliable radio and telecommunications. The Emergency Support Functions outline *which* federal agency is responsible for communications, this way, that agency could be tasked, as needed, by the incident command, to support the overall operation (DHS, 2016, p.g. 33). Other ESFs include things such as firefighting, mass care, sheltering, transportation, engineering, health and medical care, etc. Since the initial Federal Response Plan formalized the idea of the emergency support functions in the early 1990s, they have only gotten stronger in their development, and more functional. The NRF also has support annexes which describe the basic support processes specific to a number of large incident types.

National Incident Management System

An element of the NRF, includes utilizing the *National Incident Management System*, known across America to all emergency personnel and disaster planners simply as 'NIMS.' This is a communications system which is not based on electronics, but a system for personnel of one agency or multiple agencies, to speak and plan with one another during an emergency response. At each level within the incident command system (ICS), individuals that have responsibilities, and various positions which have unique responsibilities, are given distinct titles, and those titles are standardized. As the incident expands (or shrinks) those titles remain consistent even as the job responsibilities change in size—the goal is to mitigate confusion at the site of the emergency, and increase efficiency. A sample of NIMS titles include:

- Incident Commander
- Command Staff
- General Staff
- Branch / Division
- Unit

- Strike Team
- Etc.

Developed by the Department of Homeland Security in 2004, NIMS provides a uniform set of procedures for administrative, financial and support personnel, operational and logistical personnel, to the incident commanders out in the street. Using a uniform set of titles, associated responsibilities, 'plain-talk' (DHS, 2010) language, specific terminology, etc., NIMS aims to be the most efficient way to handle an incident of any type. Having different agencies all familiar with NIMS terminology and philosophy, prior to responding to an incident, can help overall incident management.

NIMS is scalable which means it can be used on a small local incident, or a large national disaster. NIMS works with the government agencies at all levels, as well as the nonprofit sector, the corporate sector, tribal governments, and private industry. The National Incident Management System (NIMS) is not necessarily a guide to emergency response, but is a type of administrative and operational management framework, which can be utilized for disasters of all types, and all sizes.

NIMS helps to coordinate communications, staff, and procedures; it works with one agency or multiple agencies, during an emergency. NIMS was initially used and implemented by the US Forest Service and the State of California to help in forest fires, however after several decades, testing, trials, and eventually through a *Homeland Security Presidential Directive* (DHS, 2003), NIMS is now used throughout the federal government, most state governments, and through a majority of smaller government elements across the United States. It's also used in corporate America, the health and medical sector, private security, etc. While there are some detractors that don't necessarily support NIMS (Bauer, 2012 & Renaud, 2016), the majority of American emergency response institutions utilize it, as does every federal agency in the United States government

Conclusion

NIMS is so important to the federal government as a central part of America's national strategy for homeland security , that FEMA has mandated that private organizations that wish to receive grants for security and emergency preparedness must educate their staff on NIMS. This generally consists of at least two specific classes that FEMA offers for free and can be taken over the internet or taught in a classroom setting, these include, *An Introduction To The Incident Command System*, and *An Introduction To The National Incident Management System* (FEMA, 2018). Such training helps an agency or organization become known as being NIMS compliant.

Among the guides, books, and manuals that the federal government has produced to lead the country through disaster planning, response, and recovery, the National Response Framework remains the key component among them. The NRF involves partnership of the government at all levels including civilians, and it looks for unity among the efforts that are put into national recovery; it prepares us as a nation to be ready to act and it remains the core document of Americas disaster and national emergency strategy.

References

Bauer, Thomas P. (2012). Is nims going to get us where we need to be? A law enforcement perspective. Center for Homeland Defense and Security: Naval Postgraduate School (U.S.), https://www.hsdl.org/?view&did=30602

DHS, (2003, Feb. 28).Homeland security presidential directive 5. U.S. Department of Homeland Security (DHS): Washington, D.C. Government Printing Office. https://www.dhs.gov/publication/ homeland-security-presidential-directive-5

DHS. (2010, June). Plain language frequently asked questions. U.S. Department of Homeland Security (DHS): Washington, D.C. Government Printing Office. https://www.dhs.gov/sites/default/files/ publications/ PlainLanguageFAQs_0.pdf (pdf)

DHS. (2016, June) National response framework. (3rd Ed.) U.S. Department of Homeland Security (DHS): Washington, D.C. Government Printing Office. https://www.fema.gov/media-library/assets/documents/117791

FEMA. (2008). National incident management system. U.S. Department of Homeland Security (DHS): Washington, D.C. Government Printing Office. https://www.fema.gov/pdf/ emergency/nims/NIMS_core.pdf (pdf).

FEMA, (2018).Implementation guidance and reporting . U.S. Department of Homeland Security (DHS): Washington, D.C. Government Printing Office. https://www.fema.gov/implementation-guidance-and-reporting

HSC. (2007, October) National strategy for homeland security. (2nd Ed.) United States Homeland Security Council (HSC): Washington, D.C. Government Printing Office. https://www.dhs.gov/national-strategy-homeland-security-october-2007

Manning, F.J., Goldfrank, L., (Eds.) (2002). Preparing for terrorism: Tools for evaluating the metropolitan medical response system program. U.S. Institute of Medicine, Committee on Evaluation of the Metropolitan Medical Response System Program. Washington, D.C.: National Academies Press.

Renaud, Cynthia E. (2016). Missing piece of nims: Teaching incident commanders how to function in the edge of chaos. Center for Homeland Defense and Security: Naval Postgraduate School (U.S.), https://www.hsaj.org/articles/221

Community Renal Dialysis Centers as Consequence Management Assets

✿ ✿ ✿

Homeland security and emergency preparedness professionals should include local dialysis centers in their community consequent management plans. This is because in the event of a massive structural collapse due to a terrorist attack or earthquake, persons trapped may develop critical injuries which require them to undergo emergency hemodialysis treatment. A surge in such patients can overwhelm a community, but may be mitigated, at least in part, through pre-established relationships with local dialysis centers that are included in community emergency plans.[50]

Background

The *U.S. Department of Homeland Security's* (DHS) *Strategic National Risk Assessment* (SNRA) addresses America's response core capabilities and identifies the threats of all hazards which may pose the greatest risk to the Nation. Among the risks and threats we are concerned with here are: 1) technological accidents and hazards to America's aging infrastructure; 2)

---

[50] The impetus for this paper came about after a casual conversation with some emergency management peers on medical emergencies flooding a community after a terrorist attack, and how the author learned those peers seemed to know little about their community dialysis centers.

events of manmade origin such as bad actors employing a Improvised Explosive Devices (IEDs); and 3) the consequences of natural hazards relating to damage from severe weather or large-scale seismic events. The common denominator of the aforementioned disasters are that they all have the potential to produce catastrophic structural collapse—with people inside them.

Introduction

A crisis condition resulting from an explosion, earthquake, or other situation, may often result in collapsed structures and associated piles of debris. Such an event may also result in trapped and injured victims unable to be rescued for some extended periods of time. The most common type of injuries sustained in a structural collapse are crushing injuries. Such injuries, whether brought about by man-made events or natural ones, are of concern to the pre-hospital, hospital and the emergency management community. Although we will briefly explain crushing injuries as a medical condition, the objective of this paper is not a lesson in medicine, but to alert the homeland security and emergency management sector to the significance of including a sometimes little-known asset of their community, the local renal dialysis centers, which should be considered in their jurisdictional consequence management plans.

Medical Syndrome

Both *Crush Injuries* and *Crush Syndrome* are traumas which directly result from having muscle compressed.[51] Compressive force on muscle is deadly, and with is comes a lethal syndrome first noted in patients who had been trapped beneath rubble of buildings in World War II. Crush Syndrome is the systemic progression of muscle cell insult ensuing from external pressure or crushing. Once the trapped victim is rescued, myoglobin (a protein found in muscle tissue) is liberated into the vascular system.[52] Myoglobin has toxic effects on the kidneys, specifically due to it blocking the renal tubules. This process known as *rhabdomyolysis*, often has the propensity to diminish flow through the kidneys, as well as subsequently reduce oxygen to the same. Ensuing complications may occur when open wounds lead to infection. The resulting sepsis can produce large quantities of inflammatory cells and toxins, which exacerbate insult to the renal tubules. Despite the fact that myoglobin is a toxic substance, renal complications occur with a physical rather than chemical effect. When severe, this syndrome may lead to Acute Renal Failure (ARF), a rapidly deadly condition.[53]

Treatment

Extensive skeletal muscle rhabdomyolysis caused by mechanical crushing must be treated early and vigorously. Since

---

[51] Antosia, R; Cahill, John D. (Eds.) *Handbook of Bioterrorism and Disaster Medicine*. Springer Science: New York, NY, 2006. 341-342

[52] Tisherman, Samuel; Forsythe, Raquel; Kellum, John A. (Eds.) *Trauma Intensive Care*. Oxford University Press: New York, NY, 2012. 115

[53] Takeda, Shinsuke et al. "Two Cases of Unidentified Acute Compartment Syndrome." *BMJ Case Reports* 2018 (2018): bcr2017222377. PMC.

rhabdomyolysis can be fatal, patients will require hemodialysis ("dialysis"), the duration of which is calculated against the severity of injury.[54] Dialysis is the process of removing toxins (as well as excess fluid) from the blood by continually circulating blood through a mechanical filtration system. It has been deduced that 30-40% of patients with rhabdomyolysis will develop Acute Renal Failure and necessitate dialysis to potentially save their lives.[55] Crushing injuries to the muscles are complicated by the amount of force applied, and the size of surface area affected. Delays in extrication and the subsequent lack of appropriate medical care can complicate matters. After the extrication of the victim—but preceding advanced clinical laboratory intervention, a simple dip-stick test in a urine sample can be used to triage those which might be developing rhabdomyolysis. However, once diagnosed, the acute rhabdomyolysis patient will require rapid dialysis.

Statistics

Crush Syndrome can be common in large earthquakes, and this condition is the second-most frequent cause of death related to earthquakes.[56] Numerous patients with this syndrome were reported after the 1976 earthquake in Tangshan, China,[57] the

---

[54] Torres, Patrick A. et al. "Rhabdomyolysis: Pathogenesis, Diagnosis, and Treatment." *The Ochsner Journal* 15.1 (2015): 58–69.

[55] Visweswaren P, Guntupalli: "Rhabdomyolysis." *Crit Care Clin* 1999; 15:415-427. Ron D, Taitelman U, Michaelson M, et al: Prevention of Acute Renal Failure in Traumatic Rhabdomyolysis. *Arch Intern Med* 1984; 144:277-280

[56] Mehmet Sukru Sever, Norbert Lameire, Raymond Vanholder, "Renal disaster relief: from theory to practice." *Nephrology Dialysis Transplantation*, Volume 24, Issue 6, June 2009, Pages 1730–1735, https://doi.org/10.1093/ndt/gfp094

[57] Zhi-Yong Z. "Medical support in the Tangshan earthquake: A review of the management of mass causalities and certain major injuries." *J Trauma* 1987; 27: 1130.

1980 earthquake in southern Italy,[58] the 1988 earthquake in Armenia,[59] the 1995 earthquake in Hanshin-Awaji, Japan,[60] and the 1999 earthquake in Marmara, Turkey.[61] The 1999 Marmara earthquake produced the largest documented nephrological emergency, with a population of over 630 patients; of these, 477 needed dialysis support. Structural collapse due to an earthquake in 2001 effected Gujarat, India. This city had one dialysis center which saw 400 chronic patients on 24 operational dialysis machines (3 daily shifts, patients dialyzed twice weekly). After the Indian disaster, medical authorities reported having 23 crush syndrome patients requiring dialysis, only later to learn there were an additional 100-150 renal failure patients at the disaster site in need of dialysis.[62]

A majority of crush injury patients developed Acute Tubular Necrosis (ATN), an irreversible condition leading to renal failure. In this care, the ATN was due a nephrotoxic syndrome, secondary to rhabdomyolysis. ATN is the most common cause of Acute Renal Failure. This same study indicated "All disaster victims with either mild or severe injuries should be followed-up closely for nephrological problems." With

---

[58] Santangelo ML, Usberti M, Di Salvo E et al. "A study of the pathology of the crush syndrome." *Surg. Gynecol. Obst.* 1982; 154: 372-4.
[59] Collins AJ. "Kidney dialysis treatment for victims of the Armenian earthquake." *N. Engl. J. Med.* 1989; 320: 1291-2.
[60] Oda J, Tanaka H, Yashioka T, et al. "Analysis of 372 patients with crush syndrome caused by the Hanshin-Awaji Earthquake." *J. Trauma* 1997; 42: 470-5.
[61] Dönmez O, Meral A, Yavuz M, Durmaz O. "Crush syndrome of children in the Marmara earthquake, Turkey." *Pediatr Intern* 2001; 43: 678-682 & Sever MS, Erek E, Vanholder R, et al. "Clinical findings in the renal victims of a catastrophic disaster: in the Marmara earthquake." *Nephrol Dial Transplant* 2002; 17: 1942-1949.
[62] International Society of Nephrology, Renal Disaster Relief Task Force, Earthquake Gujarat, India, January 26, 2001

the increasing prevalence of worldwide terrorism, communities need to prepare for ever increasing structural collapse due to terrorist events.

Community Preparedness

Throughout the U.S., homeland security professionals and emergency managers have developed plans for chronic renal patients within their jurisdictions to obtain dialysis treatments during an emergency, this is usually developed as part of a community-wide Special Needs Registry.[63] However, what communities have not done yet, is prepare for a surge load of non-pre-existing patients. Just one terrorist event can bring about a large population of sudden-need renal dialysis patients.

In developing a mass casualty dialysis plan, community preparedness should be done in concert with emergency management, local hospitals and nearby community dialysis centers. Emergency planners might want to consider developing a renal emergency team, a strategic list of contacts who have previously agreed through a memorandum of understanding or other arrangement, to respond with personnel, supplies, and if available—dialyzing machines. Such a team might be organized among organizations that exist within a specific number of miles around a geographical location. The dialysis industry is a highly organized and structured medical community, and locations of all the dialysis centers in your state can be easily obtained. The *American Association of Kidney Patients* offers a helpful device, it's

---

[63] A good source of information on emergency planning for the dialysis center is the: Chronic Kidney Disease Emergency Management Planning Guide. Ontario Renal Network. Toronto, ON, 2015. www.renalnetwork.on.ca

an online tool to locate dialysis centers anywhere from 5-100 miles from a specific zip code. Contingencies may also include plans for dialysis patients (both pre-existing chronic and newly trauma-induced ones) to be evacuated out of the area, or for calling up a renal emergency team which may rely on assets such as mobile dialysis vans and other resources.

National Response

If a major terrorist incident brought down a large building, there theoretically could be a large number of survivors requiring dialysis, overwhelming most communities. The U.S. departments of *Homeland Security* and *Health and Human Services* has assets within the *National Disaster Medical System (NDMS)*, which can be deployed within 12-24 hours to provide 60-member *Disaster Medical Assistance Teams (DMAT)* anywhere in the country. However, while such teams exist (and there are also specialized teams such a veterinary and mortuary teams), there is no federal specialty hemodialysis team. With the continued threat of terror, and recent increased seismic activity in the United States, it may be a prudent idea for the U.S. government to assemble a renal emergency team. This would be a highly mobile medical team equipped with mobile dialysis machines which could respond to man-made disasters.[64]

A renal emergency team has already been developed by the Belgium-*based International Society of Nephrology*. Their *Renal*

---

[64] As one resource, see the *Centers for Medicare & Medicaid Services* (CMS) which regulates the *End Stage Renal Disease* program, a division of the *U.S. Department of Health and Human Services* (DHHS). The DHHS is the same federal executive agency which operates the *Office of Emergency Preparedness*, tasked with emergency medical (consequence management) after a terrorist attack.

Disaster Relief Task Force exists to provide renal care in the aftermath of large natural and human-made catastrophes.[65] Though this organization is not based in the United States, it might be prudent for those who plan for contingencies to contact this organization for advice on putting together a renal emergency team.[66]

Conclusion

Generally, dialysis for those with chronic renal disease is conducted in hospitals, at specialized healthcare and medical centers ("dialysis centers") and can be done at home through the care of mobile dialysis services. These community-based dialysis centers should be part of a community's consequent management plans; just as any good community homeland security / emergency management plan will pre-assess the number of hospital beds that are generally available locally—the number of dialysis beds should be queried as well.

A comprehensive plan which could best deal with a surge in Crush Syndrome patients resulting from a man-made, technological or natural caused situation, would benefit from a relationship established between emergency management and community dialysis centers, public and private. These centers should be invited participants in community-wide disaster drills, just as hospitals are. A strong relationship between the homeland security / emergency management team and dialysis centers can

---

[65] It should be noted some hemodialysis equipment manufacturers have indeed responded with staff and equipment to states affected by disasters such as hurricanes, to assist chronic dialysis patients.

[66] See https://www.nature.com/articles/ncpneph0862.pdf

help a community meet an unexpected surge of patients in the event of an emergency of any type. On a national level, there remains a need to rapidly deploy nephrologists, specially trained nursing staff, and dialysis technicians, as well as sufficient supplies—all which can make the difference in survival.

A key takeaway for emergency preparedness professionals, is to note that approximately 50% of the patients with Crush Syndrome develop Acute Renal Failure and approximately 50% of those will need swift dialysis;[67] for this reason, communities need to be prepared to handle large scale dialysis surge emergencies.

---

[67] Erek E, Sever MS, Serdengeçti K, et al. An overview of morbidity and mortality in patients with acute renal failure due to crush syndrome: the Marmara earthquake experience. *Nephrol Dial Transplant* 2002; 17: 33-40.

Presidential Executive Orders and America's National Disaster Management

✧ ✧ ✧

A n Executive Order (EO) is a hand-signed directive issued by the President of the United States, much like other means of presidential direct action which includes not only executive orders, but also national security directives, national disaster declarations, and presidential proclamations. Yet, while there are several means of presidential direct action, it is the Executive Order which holds the most weight. EO's have the force of law. They are legal directives that help manage operations of the federal government. These signed orders are often used to rapidly put in place a measure or action which would usually have taken quite a long time to employ if the same idea was sent through Congress for the traditional approval process approval. This paper examines the history of the presidential Executive Orders, how they have enhanced national disaster response and recovery, and will demonstrate how EOs have contributed to enhancing the resilience strategy for national disaster management.

Introduction

In June of 1789, while the Russo-Turkish War was actively being fought, and the French Revolution had just been sparked, the United States was still enjoying a period of tranquillity which arrived after a long and brutal war for independence some three years earlier.[68] It was the summer of 1789, and President George Washington had been in office for only a few months—almost a full year before the ratification of the new Constitution. President Washington sent a directive in writing to John Jay,[69] who at the time was Secretary of Foreign Affairs for the existing government of the Confederation of states. Washington wanted to learn what was going on in different avenues of the rapidly changing government, when he directed Jay to send him in writing, "a clear account of the Department" he was at the head of "...impress me with a full, precise & distinct general idea of the United States."[70] This directive dispatched directly from the president to one of his cabinet members with a direct request for action is considered by law scholars as the first executive order from a president.[71]

Every president has issued Executive Orders, with the exception of William Harrison who only served for a month in office before succumbing to pneumonia. The Commander-in-Chief who signed the most EO's was Franklin Delano Roosevelt (3738), history remembers this most notably, because the country was at war, and, FDR served the country longer than any other president. FDR signed 3738 Executive Orders; in

---

[68] Glenn Moots, "Guest Editor's Introduction: The American Revolution 240 Years Later: Was It a Just War?, *Journal of Military Ethics*, 14:1, 3-6, DOI: 10.1080/15027570.2015.1033891 .

[69] Lindsay Chervinsky, "The historical presidency: George Washington and the First Presidential Cabinet. *Presidential Studies Quarterly, 48*(1), (2018): 139-152.

[70] Letter from George Washington to John Jay, 8 June 1789.

[71] Harold C. Relye, "Presidential Directives: Background and Overview." *CRC*

Congressional Report for Congress #98-611, (Nov. 11, 2008), 5.

recent years, President Bill Clinton signed 364, George W. Bush, 291, and Barak Obama 276.[72]

Executive Orders are used by presidents for various reasons, sometimes to implement policy by use of a pen and without the Congress:

> In 1793, President George Washington issued an executive order declaring American neutrality in the war between France and England. At the time, Washington's order was seen as a pro-British move, since the 1788 Treaty with France required the colonies to defend French interests in North America. Washington's use of an executive order was a strategic choice, as he believed that Congress was unlikely to embrace his position.[73] This was not the last time that a President used an executive order to accomplish policy goals.[74]

President Donald Trump has been spoken of negatively for using his EO power, but such accusations occurred with President Obama too. When Executive Orders are utilized the political shadow of polarization often becomes involved.[75] Yet, many on both sides of the aisle know that good can come from an EO, and the public knows this as well. Of course, nothing in Washington DC comes without some degree of expressed commentary or

---

[72] Gerhard Peters & John T. Woolley, "Executive Orders." *The American Presidency Project.* ed. John T. Woolley and Gerhard Peters. Santa Barbara, CA: U.C. Santa Barbara, 1999-2018.
http://www.presidency.ucsb.edu/data/orders.php.
[73] Richard M. Pious, *The American Presidency.* New York: Basic Books, (1979): 51
[74] Derring, Christopher J. and Forrest Maltzman. 1999. 767-768
[75] S. Q. Kelly, "The Preeminence of Politics: Executive Orders from Eisenhower to Clinton." *Choice,* Vol 45, no. 9. (May 2008): 1619.

opinion, but for the most part, EO's issued related to organizing the federal government to better prepare, respond and recover from disasters of all types, is generally something people have agreed upon.

Presidential Executive Orders as Facilitators

President Richard Nixon

Between 1960-1970, several large disasters affected the U.S. which required enormous federal response. These disasters brought much needed attention on the issue of federal response to national disasters and resulted in improved regulations and increased legislature in the area of emergency and disaster management. In 1969 President Richard Nixon issued Executive Order 11495[76] which provided for the administration of *his Disaster Relief Act of 1969*, this was a financial grant program for communities stricken by a disaster. The following year, Nixon issued EO 11575, which formalized his initial *Disaster Relief Act*.[77] This EO provided a focus on four key items: 1) To provide a tax plan for local governments whose jurisdiction have been affected or destroyed during a disaster, 2) To provide the legal ability to replace damaged government facilities, 3) To better the Federal loan programs for people affected by disasters, and 4) Create a legal program to help States and local governments to provide hazard mitigation development plans. "The bill demonstrates that the Federal Government in cooperation with State and local

---

[76] November 18, 1969
[77] Public Law 91606

authorities is capable of providing compassionate assistance to the innocent victims of natural disasters" President Nixon said.[78]

Several catastrophic disasters struck the United States in the early 1970's. In 1971 the San Fernando Earthquake toppled buildings and freeways in California. In 1972, Hurricane Agnes struck the eastern seaboard, vanquishing the railroad infrastructure, killing over 100 and becoming the costliest natural disaster with $2.1 billion (12.6 billion in 2018) in damages. The following year flooding along the Mississippi River occurred— the third most severe floods of the 20th century. President Nixon lamented:

> During the past four years, we have tried to reduce personal injury, deaths, and property damage by emphasizing adequate preventive measures. During the same period, however, I've had to declare 111 major disasters in 39 States and three territories. This past year alone set a tragic record for major disaster activity....[79]

In 1974, in response to the major disasters which had struck the country, the President and the legislature bolstered national disaster response by signing EO 11795, which solidified the procedure of the President making disaster declarations. President Nixon went on to institute the *Disaster Relief Act of 1974*.[80] The Act covered the 50 states, the District of Colombia, and American territories in the Atlantic and Pacific. The Act had seven core elements all based around disaster preparedness and

---

[78] Nixon, 1970.
[79] Nixon, 1975, pg. 779
[80] Public Law 93-288

recovery, they included: 1) Revised and broadened the scope of existing disaster relief programs, 2) Encouraged the development of comprehensive preparedness plans by State and local governments, 3) A desire to achieve greater coordination and responsiveness, 4) Encouraged States and local governments to obtain insurance coverage, 5) Encouraged hazard mitigation, 6) Provided Federal assistance programs to cover both public and private loses, and 7) Develop a long-term economic recovery program for major disasters. This revised Act also introduced grants of up to $250,000 to States and local governments for disaster preparedness and planning.

In regard to disaster resilience, Nixon's Executive Orders in both 1970 and 1974, helped spark an amalgamation of the Federal government with State and local governments like never before. While the States were tasked in creating mitigation plans and other disaster preparedness programs, they were also remunerated through grants and promises of support and commitment in the event a disaster strikes one of their communities. Uncle Sam would be there for them, all they had to do was participate in the advance planning which would help make States and local communities increasingly resilient. Executive Order 11795 and its associated *Disaster Relief Act of 1974,* was a strong step in the right direction for post-war modern emergency management.

Formalizing and Clarifying Response & Recovery Efforts

President Jimmy Carter

In the summer of 1978, President Jimmy Carter wrote to Congress about reorganizing federal response to the nation's disasters, both because he saw the tragedy disasters had caused, and by hearing the calls for reorganization by state governors.[81] Thirteen months later, the President signed Executive Order 12148 into law on July 20, 1979 creating the Federal Emergency Management Agency (FEMA), and months later Congress provided its blessing.

FEMA was born by consolidating many different acts, laws, and executive orders—as well revoking numerous executive orders,[82] some of these pertained to the *National Security Act of 1947; the Federal Civil Defense Act of 1950; the Defense Production Act of 1950; the Strategic and Critical Materials Stock Piling Act of 1950; the Disaster Relief Act of 1970;* and *the Earthquake Hazards Reduction Act of 1977.* EO 12148 brought together federal agencies responsible for emergency preparedness and civil defense, now placing them under one umbrella that would be the lead consequence management agency for presidentially-declared disasters or civil emergency, including any "accidental, natural, man-caused, or wartime emergency or threat thereof, which causes or may cause substantial injury or harm to the population or substantial damage to or loss of property."[83]

---

[81] Patrick Roberts, "FEMA After Katrina." Policy Review. Hoover Institution. Stanford University: Stanford, CA. (2006, June 1)
https://www.hoover.org/research/fema-after-katrina
[82] Dave Ross, "Explanation of Proposed Amendments to Executive Order 12148, Federal Emergency Management., (June 1998): 1-44. Washington D.C.: Federation of American Scientists. https://fas.org/irp/agency/dhs/fema/
[83] EO 12148 2-203

At the time, preparing for and responding to both man-made and natural disasters, was the responsibility of several different federal agencies. Up until 1980, the primary federal agencies for this mission was the *Defense Civil Preparedness Agency* (DCPA)—a division of *the Department of Defense* (DOD), and the *Federal Disaster Assistance Administration* (FDAA)—a body within the *Department of Housing and Urban Development* (HUD). Both of these large agencies shared the role of fulfilling national preparedness strategies. In total, there existed over 30 different agencies all with a role to play in national preparedness and response. With the stroke of his pen on the bottom of EO 12148, President Jimmy Carter's begun a major sea change in overall American disaster resilience.

President George H.W. Bush

President Bush amended Executive Order 12148 in 1988, expanding President Nixon's earlier *Disaster Relief Act*, and providing FEMA with a more robust statutory authority for overall response to national disasters. The law is known as the *Robert T. Stafford Disaster Relief and Emergency Assistance Act*, named in honor of Robert Stafford (1913-2006), former Congressman, Senator and Governor of the state of Vermont, who had served as a Naval officer in WWII and Korea. The Act provided an orderly and methodical way for the government to assist State and local governments during a disaster. The Act also provides funds to relocate people, provides protection for structures that have not yet been damaged, and provides hazard mitigate grants to help prepare against future disasters. Bush's EO formalized this system of providing both fiscal and logistical assistance to State (and local) governments, and was a positive change for the emergency management sector.

Executive Order 12148 said when a State became overwhelmed by a disaster of such a magnitude that it can no longer handle the situation effectively, the governor of that State will reach out to the Federal government for assistance, namely the Regional FEMA representative. This is typically done by a phone call and followed-up with a written request (Bazan, 2006). The overall disaster situation is then rapidly evaluated by federal authorities, and if it's considered severe enough, the President signs a declaration recognizing the disaster situation as valid and with that appoints a federal coordinating officer (FCO) to the State. The FCO then assists in making a wide range of federal resources (cash, supplies, logistical support for transportation, etc.) available to assist the State in dealing with both the disaster crisis, and subsequent consequences.

America's Most Recent National Disasters

It is not only the President of the United States that has executive authority. Among the states, the chief executive, the Governor, has the ability to issue Executive Orders. Such EO's carry the weight of law throughout the state, in a similar vein as the President does through his national Executive Orders. We saw this after Hurricane Andrew. In the fall of 1992, the United States took a severe blow, Hurricane Andrew struck Florida causing over $25 billion dollars in damage. Andrew produced widespread catastrophic damage to South Florida and created a homelessness problem for tens of thousands of Americans; the storm destroyed or damaged over 750,000 buildings. Following disasters such as this, a governor can issue an EO. This is what Florida's Governor Lawton Chiles did; he issued Executive Order 92-242 which established a state-wide disaster committee which would bring in experts to assess the situation associated with that catastrophic disaster.[84] This case in a good example of how a state (or the federal government) can immediately put the wheels in motion for something which is time sensitive, such as putting together an investigative committee. If the assembly of a committee such as this was to be implemented the traditional way of being established by legislature, it could take many months before the committee would even be launched. This case is a simple but effective way to illustrate how an EO can rapidly be a catalyst for an important action.

President Jimmy Carter's EO 12148 (1979) launched FEMA and Bush's subsequent EO 12148 (1988), implemented the Stafford Act. Both of these EO's where designed originally to deal with natural disasters. But it wasn't until the 1990's that FEMA adopted an "all-hazards" approach to dealing with emergencies. This meant that FEMA would prepare to respond to all disasters, whether they were natural, man-made or technological in nature.

The attacks on the United States which occurred on September 11th, 2001, changed everything about modern emergency management, this occurred with President Bush's 2001 EO 13228 which established the Department of Homeland Security, (DHS), which brought together over 20 federal

---

[84] Mittler, Elliott. "A Case Study of Florida's Emergency Management Since Hurricane Andrew. *Natural Hazards Research and Applications Information."* University of Colorado Boulder. (1997) https://hazdoc.colorado.edu/handle/10590/1922 Vol. 70., No. 213.

government agencies into that single organization. One of the agencies that was brought under the wings of DHS, was the Federal Emergency Management agency.

In 2005, Hurricane Katrina struck the U.S. causing a disastrous situation along the Gulf Coast from Texas to Florida. The storm surge and severe flooding led to 1,800 deaths, and cost taxpayers over $125 billion dollars. This storm was a nightmare to all who participated in the rescue and recovery efforts. Following Katrina, President Bush issued two EO's, 13389 and 13390, these assisted with disaster recovery, by creating the Gulf Coast Recovery and Rebuilding Council and the establishment of a Coordinator of Federal Support for the Recovery and Rebuilding of the Gulf Coast Region.[85]

Conclusion

Only the major EO's have been touched on heretofore, but a more extensive examination of the literature would focus on other EO's and their outcomes which made strides to better our resilience strategy for national disasters. This includes President John Kennedy's 1962 EO's 10997, 10998, 10999, 11000, 11001, 11002, 11003, 11004 and 11005, which assigned emergency preparedness functions to several federal executive offices including the Secretary of Agriculture, Secretary of Commerce, Secretary of Labor, Secretary of Health, Education, and Welfare, the postmaster General, the Administrator of the Federal Aviation Agency, the Housing and Home Finance Administrator, and the Interstate Commerce Commission. Further, EO 11310 (1966) assigned emergency preparedness

---

[85] *Federal Register* Part VI November 4, 2005

duties to the Office of the US Attorney General; EO 11988 (1977) signed by Jimmy Carter addressed floodplain management; EO 12472 (1984) signed by Ronald Reagan which enhanced national emergency telecommunications preparedness; and EO 12657 which provided for emergency planning at commercial nuclear energy generating facilities.

Over the decades the presidential use of the Executive Order has enhanced national disaster response and recovery. Today, after a major disaster, when something must be done, it's not uncommon for a president to use the power of an EO to get that mission complete. The use of an Executive Order is faster than going through the legislative process, and as long as it's not setting major national policies on issues that are hot to either Republicans or Democrats, Executive Orders are usually met with little push back or negative comments. This is especially true during a situation of a national emergency or after a disaster. The Executive Order has become an essential part of our national strategy for types of disasters. In the future, I'm sure Executive Orders will continue to be used for the same reasons, enhancing disaster recovery and response.

References

E. B. Bazan, "Robert T. Stafford Disaster Relief and Emergency Assistance Act: Legal Requirements for Federal and State Roles in Declarations of an Emergency or a Major Disaster. CRC Report for Congress RL-33090, (2006, September 16). Congressional Research Service. The Library of Congress: Washington, D.C.

Lindsay M. Chervinsky, "The Historical Presidency: George Washington and the First Presidential Cabinet." *Presidential Studies Quarterly, 48*(1), (2018): 139-152. doi:http://dx.doi.org.ezproxy1.apus.edu/10.1111/psq.12387

Christopher J. Derring, & Forrest Maltzman, "The Politics of Executive Orders: Legislative Constraints on Presidential Power. *Political Research Quarterly*, 52(4), (1999): 767-783. doi:http://dx.doi.org.ezproxy1.apus.edu/10.1177/106591299905200405

Executive Order 12148--Federal Emergency Management (Jimmy Carter - July 20, 29178) (44 FR 43239, 3 CFR, 1979 Comp., p. 412)

Federal Register. Part VI (November 4, 2005).

FEMA. "FEMA Can Improve Its Learning from Past Experience and Management of Disaster-Related Resources." *GAO Report to Congress 08-301* (February 2008): 1-30 https://www.gao.gov/products/GAO-08-301

FEMA. "Needs Adequate Data, Plans, and Systems to Effectively Manage Resources for Day-to-Day Operations." *GAO Report to Congress 07-139* (January 2007): 1-38 https://www.gao.gov/products/GAO-07-139

S. Q. Kelly, "The Preeminence of Politics: Executive Orders from Eisenhower to Clinton." *Choice* 45, no. 9 (05, 2008): 1619, https://search-proquest-com.ezproxy1.apus.edu/docview/225729818?accountid=8289.

Elliot Mittler, "A Case Study of Florida's Emergency Management Since Hurricane Andrew." *Natural Hazards Research and Applications Information*. University of Colorado Boulder. (1997) https://hazdoc.colorado.edu/handle/10590/1922 Vol. 70., No. 213.

Glenn Moots, "Guest Editor's Introduction: The American Revolution 240 Years Later: Was It a Just War?, *Journal of Military Ethics*, 14:1, (May 15, 2015): 3-6, DOI: 10.1080/15027570.2015.1033891 .

Richard Nixon, "Statement on signing the disaster relief act of 1970.," Online by Gerhard Peters and John T. Woolley, *The American Presidency Project*. (1970, December 31). http://www.presidency.ucsb.edu/ws/?pid=2875.

Richard Nixon, "Public Papers of The Presidents of The United States: Richard M. Nixon, 1973. Washington: Office of the Federal Register, National Archives and Records Service, General Services Administration: Washington, D.C. (1975).

Glenn A. Phelps, "George Washington and the Founding of the Presidency." *Presidential Studies Quarterly* 17, no. 2 (1987): 345-63. http://www.jstor.org/stable/40574456.

Public Law 91606: Disaster Relief Act of 1970. Government Printing Office.

Public Law 93-288: Disaster Relief Act of 1974. Government Printing Office.

Yvonne Rademacher, "Outcontracting in Emergency Management: More than a Business Conundrum." *International Journal of Disaster Risk Science* (December) 2, no. 4: 15-21. https://doi.org/10.1007/s13753-011-0016-5

Harold C. Relye, "Presidential Directives: Background and Overview." *CRC Congressional Report for Congress #98-611*, (Nov. 11, 2008), 5.

Richard M. Pious, *The American Presidency*. New York: Basic Books, 1979.

Andrew Reeves, "Political Disaster: Unilateral Powers, Electoral Incentives, and Presidential Disaster Declarations." *The Journal of Politics*, 73, no. 4. (October 2011): 1142-1151. doi=10.1017/S0022381611000843

Patrick Roberts, "FEMA After Katrina." *Policy Review*. Hoover Institution. Stanford University: Stanford, CA. (2006, June 1) https://www.hoover.org/research/fema-after-katrina

Dave Ross, "Explanation of Proposed Amendments to Executive Order 12148, Federal Emergency Management., (June 1998): 1-44. Washington D.C.: Federation of American Scientists. https://fas.org/irp/agency/dhs/fema/

Richard T. Sylves, "Coping with Catastrophe: Building an Emergency Management System to Meet People's Needs in Natural and Manmade Disasters." *Public Administration Review*, vol. 54, no. 3, (1994): pp. 303-307. Academic OneFile

Richard Sylves & William R. Cumming, "FEMA's Path to Homeland Security: 1979-2003." *Journal of Homeland Security and Emergency Management*, 1(2) (2004): doi:10.2202/1547-7355.1023

Gary L. Wamsley, & Aaron D. Schroeder, "Escalating in a Quagmire: The Changing Dynamics of the Emergency Management Policy Subsystem." *Public Administration Review*, 56, no. 3, (1996): 235-44. doi:10.2307/976446.

George Washington, "Letter from George Washington to John Jay, 8 June 1789," Founders Online, National Archives, last modified June 13, 2018, http://founders.archives.gov/documents/Washington/05-02-02-0335. [Original source: The Papers of George Washington, Presidential Series, vol. 2, 1 April 1789–15 June 1789, ed. Dorothy Twohig. Charlottesville: University Press of Virginia, 1987, p. 455.]

Homegrown Violent Extremism and Their Use of Social Media

✿ ✿ ✿

Homegrown violent extremism has been an increasing problem in North America, over the last couple of decades. For many years we have looked at homegrown extremists as mostly people with causes that are related to American domestic issues like the environment, animal rights, abortion issues, etc. Yet, these days we know that even homegrown actors often will take upon themselves, special and political issues that have their roots in foreign causes. However, whether the cause the extremist takes up is domestic or foreign, they usually are associated with violence and disruption in the same manner.

Background

The extremist(s) desire to commit chaos. They desire to break down law and order and put fear into the hearts of those they seek attention from. While some homegrown violent extremists (HVEs) act alone, other homegrown extremists work with others, fighting (in their minds) for a common cause. Whether it is an animal rights group attempting to liberate confined animals, or a group rallying to save trees, or stop an oil pipeline—in a civilized society, there should never be any excuse for using violence.

The HVE groups which work together to fight for their causes, used to find each other on school campuses, through flyers, and club meetings, etc.; then they found each other on computer bulletin boards in the 1980's and early 1990's. Then by the mid 1990's up until today, they have used the various social media platforms to express their feelings and to recruit others. The impact social media platforms have had on homegrown extremists is incredible. Social media allows people to talk to others and to get their message out to others, exponentially.

Platforms such as *Twitter*, allows people to talk to others they do not know, and *Facebook*, which for the most part is for continuing conversations with people and groups you do know, are two of the largest social platforms. These are used to communicate with others, to share viewpoints, and to ultimately can be used to inspire others. Other social media platforms like the extremely popular *Whatsapp*, provides point-to-point encryption (Ranger, 2017) for all text, photos and voice messages; this provides a layer of security for those groups who want to keep away from law enforcement.

This is not just about domestic individuals and groups, social media is being leveraged by international groups as well. This includes Mexican cartels, and the HVE who may be an American-born person who has taken it upon himself to join a radical Islamic group which is overseas, but is operating domestically as a potential one wolf; this may even be someone that desires to hoist the Islamic battle flag over an American city. Those Jihad-oriented HVEs are just as serious in their intentions as the domestic cause (abortion, animals, environment) HVEs. What is common about both groups, is that when they feel a need to share their points of view, or to mingle with others of the same breed, they can go online and use social media to find friends who espouse similar interests.

Radicalization may be initiated when a set of grievances is spoken, and can end with a path of violence; the radicalization process may start as something as simple as a complaint and end with an ideology. Social media can be the catalyst for this, a vehicle for this. The sharing of words, ideas and especially videos, can put an enormous amount of influence on someone—and this does not need to be religious-based. The impact of the internet and social media on North American homegrown extremism has been enormous. The fact that the HVEs can "fly under the radar" nowadays using encrypted communications is a major obstacle for law enforcement. The US Department of Homeland Security says, "The use of the Internet and social media to recruit and radicalize individuals to violence means that conventional approaches are unlikely to identify and disrupt all terrorist plots" (DHS, 2017, pg. 1). Social media has become the de facto home port in the sea of HVE discussions. Still, not only are these radicals using online services to recruit and `radicalize others, in doing so they are leaving a nourishing trail of forensic data for the criminal investigator (Siegel & Mirakovits, 2015, pg. 183). If there is a "good" side it is that many crimes have been solved, and people have been located through the use of social media and the internet.

The US Department of Homeland Security (DHS) and the Federal Bureau of Investigation (FBI) are the two top law enforcement agencies in the US, who face the realities of dealing with the HVE on a daily basis. This includes not only the

American-born bad actors with a domestic cause célèbre, but the Islamic religious based HVEs who have been radicalized and now desire to fight the west—in the west. The US Intelligence Community's *Worldwide Threat Assessment* (WTA), says that homegrown violent extremists (HVEs) will remain the "most frequent and unpredictable" Islamic extremist threat to the US homeland.

There have been many efforts to counter homegrown violent extremists in North America. A few years ago, the Obama White House hosted a Summit on Countering Violent Extremism which focused on both domestic and foreign terrorism. Soon after the Justice Department announced a new anti-terrorism initiative, known as Countering Violent Extremism (CVE). This program desired to deter U.S. residents from joining "violent extremist" groups. The strategy was they would bring community and religious leaders together, with law enforcement and the medical community, as well as social workers of all types. The CVE pilot programs were for Boston, Los Angeles, and Minneapolis. In FY2015, Boston, Massachusetts received a total of $23,600,000 from FEMA, Los Angeles, California received $130,000,000, and Minneapolis, Minnesota got $9,500,000 for their CVE programs.[86]

---

[86] Freedom of Information Act Request from Meghan Koushik, Research & Programs Associate, and Michael Price, Counsel, Brennan Center for Justice to the Records Management/Disclosure Branch, Federal Emergecy Management Agency FOIA Office, concerning grant applications submitted by the State of California, the State of Massachusetts, and the State of Minnesota to the Homeland Security Grant Program (HSGP) for Fiscal Year (FY) 2015 (June 30, 2015).

Unfortunately, there has not been much positive news on these programs. "The programs include attempts, with no basis in evidence, to predict who might some day become violent due to a passionate investment in a cause" said LoCicero and Boyd. Some called it exploitation of community outreach for intelligence purposes. And the news is filled with stories on how these CVE programs are really there to "spy" on communities.

I feel the truth is, deradicalization programs, whether for domestic or foreign radicals, just don't work. I have not read one positive manner in which it can be done, and then repeated. It may take many years for a plan to be devised on how to counter violent extremism, if one can be developed at all. The American government threw a lot of money against the wall, and hoped something would stick, but it does not seem like that has happened. The homegrown terrorists in Boston acted in their stated love of Islam and against America—their own country. Until we, Americans, can come up with a plan to make our children love us more than foreign ideas, we may never make a change. Those brothers chose their religion over their country. I'm not sure how this can be countered, as religion is such a strong attraction to many, being born into it.

References

Brennan Center. (2017). Countering violent extremism: Freedom of information law requests. NY, NY NYC School of Law. https://www.brennancenter.org/analysis/countering-violent-extremism-freedom-information-law-requests

DHS. (2017). Terrorism prevention partnerships. GPO: Washington, DC. www.dhs.gov/terrorism-prevention-partnerships

LoCicero, A; Boyd, W. (2016, July 19). The dangers of countering violent extremism (CVE): Programs. *Psychology Today.* *www.psychologytoday.com/blog/almost-addicted/201607/*

Ranger, S. (2017, March 27). The uncrackable problem of end-to-end encryption. ZDnet. http://www.zdnet.com/article/the-uncrackable-problem-of-end-to-end-encryption/

Scaife, L. Social networks as the new frontier of terrorism: #Terror.

Siegel, J.A; Mirakovits, K. (2015). Forensic science: The basics. Boca Raton, FL: CRC Press.

Directed Patrol, and its Success in America's Largest Police Department

✧ ✧ ✧

As police science evolved in the 20th century, many different tactics and procedures were proposed and introduced. Among them was the 'problem-oriented policing.' This was a reactive way of running a department, which has the officers chasing after crimes as crimes were committed. Another method, one which was more pro-active in nature, was the 'directed patrol,' a form of patrol that involved concentrating the police presence in an area where crime had gotten to be a significant problem. In New York City, where America's largest police department was hard at work fighting a severe crime plague in the 1980s, an introduction of directed patrol was one of the many successful tactics which helped the crime rate plunge. This paper will introduce directed patrols, their political ramifications, their tactical usage, and how overall, they were a positive help in the city's crime rate dropping by some 68% between 1980-2016.

If one was to explain a major difference in two popular styles of policing, it would be the difference between being reactive vs. pro-active. A great example of that is the difference between problem-oriented policing (POP) and directed patrols (DP). In problem-oriented policing, the problem is the protagonist in the police equation. The problem is what draws the police to the scene of the crime. The term *problem-oriented policing* was coined back in 1979, when it was seen as a scientific approach for the police business (Bullock & Tilly, 2012).

In 1994, at the peak of New York City's ongoing two-decades long malaise, Rudy Giuliani was elected Mayor, and with him came the newly appointed Police Commissioner, William Bratton, who was previously the Transit Police Chief (Barajas, 2014, pg.46). Bratton inherited a crime-ridden, hollowed out New York City where crime was ubiquitous and stopping it would be an uphill battle. Bratton utilized problem-oriented policing, like most departments did. His most effective yet controversial action, was the implementation of the "broken windows" theory of crime fighting. Broken windows demonstrated that small crimes which affect quality of life needed to be addressed. If the windows in the neighborhood were broken—soon other windows would be broken. The allegory said people must not care about the neighborhood, so a spiral of downward crimes would continue to occur, in number and magnitude. Yet, that wouldn't happen. Bratton, with Giuliani's support, changed the culture of the NYPD, and brought broken windows policing and other crime-fighting techniques to the center. Bratton saw crime like this: Disorder --> Citizen Fear --> Withdrawal (Physical & Social) --> Increased Predatory Behavior --> Increased Predatory Behavior --> Increased Crime --> Spiral of Decline (Kelling & Bratton, 1998, pg. 1219)

Bratton wanted his officers to be "more assertive in their enforcement of minor offenses" (Sousa, 2010, pg.45). No matter what the anti-institutionalists said, the seemingly minor quality of life calls were responded to, and the perpetrators were arrested and sentenced for their crimes, no matter how small they were. Not only did he push this forward in the department, but he also brought forward the idea of computerizing the crime statistics, and this evolved into the CompStat program. Having weekly and monthly crime stats, allowed the department brass to hold the precincts more accountable. Insomuch, the stats also held the brass accountable themselves. It was during this era in the NYPD history, that accountability became paramount—for both the precinct level bosses, and the top brass. The CompStat data reported numerous variables, but one of the most prominent was 'where' the crimes were being repeatedly committed.

Being increasing pro-active, Commissioner Bratton took that location-based data, and sent his officers to those locations; he sent them randomly and he sent them on a schedule. Known as directive patrols (DP), this style of policing was one of the "modern" police strategies of the 1990s (Fritsch, et al., 2009, pg.99). DP came about after the successful experimental usage of new police procedures in Kansas City in 1992. In 1997, directed patrols were successfully featured in a program in Indianapolis, (US DOJ, 1999, pg. 70) from this, through conferences, articles and discussion, directed patrol became a popular police practice.

Directed patrols were a proactive strategy that actively sought out criminal acts in areas which have been identified as hot spots of criminal activity. Identifying these locations, and sending in officers in a more assertive (aka aggressive) manner, results in increased arrests. Not only inside their regular patrol areas, but DPs are conducted by the Hercules teams, the heavy weapons special operations teams which visit and patrol strategically important locations such as museums, landmarks, transit hubs, etc. The teams are assigned based on intelligence data, and aim to become a disruption to terrorists who may be surveilling or planning something.

Statistics

Directed patrols was a large part of that which changed the NYPD and the culture of the police department in general. Going from a reactive force, to one which went after the crime and put criminals on the offensive was possibly one of the best things the city ever saw. Misdemeanor arrests increased 70% in New York City over the 1990s and the prison population rose 24%. Crime was falling fast in the 1990s, when the *New York Times* reported:

> Murders, which had been falling gradually over the previous three years, dropped sharply, by nearly a fifth, in 1994. Overall, 350 fewer people were slain in 1994 than in the year before, and 650 fewer than in 1990, when murders, many of them fueled by the crack epidemic, reached a peak (Krauss, 1995, 12).

The crime rate drops which were scene in New York City startled the nation. Their crime rate dropped twice as fast as the average, and it played out in the media, with lots of reports in the papers and on the nightly news. At the present time, crime seems to be dropping again, and it is if you believe in the crime statistics and what the Mayor's office reports. The use of directed patrols, a solid part of daily life within the NYPD, and certainly these continue to help lower the crime rate.

Discussion

For this paper I had a short discussion with Glen Schneider, a 29-year veteran of the NYPD, and currently the Highway 5 Auxiliary Lieutenant-in-Command. Schneider discussed how currently, directed patrols are made at any location which needs a more intense police presence. This can be at train stations, where often a pair of officers will wait for a train to arrive and depart, they will walk through the train, to allow the passengers to see them, then they will exit the train and patrol the platform. Sometimes they may ride the train up and back a station. Directed patrols are often done in response to previous problems at houses of worship, and these often involve not just visiting the location or passing by, but stopping and speaking with the clergy. Of course, this is a classic community affairs type role, and can only strengthen the bond between the local officers and the clergy. Officer Schneider informed me that police officers may conduct directed patrols as much as once an hour, and the patrols themselves can be conducted in a vehicle, but more often involve walking. "A DP can take anywhere from 5-7 minutes, to up to an hour sometimes—you never know what's gonna be." Schneider advised that when a crime is found during a directed patrol, they are mandated to document that crime did indeed occur (or was founded) during the patrol—this is done over the radio; this allows NYPD's CompStat program to be on top of the numbers. Not only are directed patrols an important set of figures to maintain, but the NYPD prides itself on them, so you can imagine how important they are.

Conclusion

Directed patrols were something new when they started—and nothing is easy when it comes to change, especially in a police department that has stout roots, going back some 172 years. DPs remain today, and are part of the daily culture of the police department. Now, some two decades after they were implemented, some police officers don't even remember before they DP existed. Just recently, NYPD officers on a directed patrol ended up saving the life of a young man who overdosed. They gave him Narcan because they found him on a directed patrol, which if they had not been on, he'd probably never survive (Ostapiuk, 2017, pg. 1).

References

Barajas, Ed. (2014). The quiet revolution: Shattering the myths about the American criminal justice system. Bloomington, IN: iUniverse.

Bullock, K; Tilly, N. (Eds). (2012). Crime reduction and problem-oriented policing. NY, NY: Routledge .

Fritsch, E. J., Liederbach, J., Taylor, R. W., & Caeti, M. (2009). Police patrol allocation and deployment. Upper Saddle River, NJ: Prentice Hall.

Kelling, G.L., & Bratton, W.J. (1998). Declining crime rates: Insiders' views of the New York City story. Journal of Criminal Law & Criminology, 88(4), 1217-1231. Retrieved from https://search-proquest-com.ezproxy2.apus.edu/docview/218440130?accountid=8289

Krauss, C. (1995, January 1). New York City crime falls but just why is a mystery. http://www.nytimes.com/1995/01/01/nyregion/new-york-city-crime-falls-but-just-why-is-a-mystery.html?pagewanted=all

Ostapiuk, J. (2017, December 8). NYPD touts Narcan save at Old Town train station. NY: Staten Island Live.

Schneider, G. (2018, January 15). Oral Interview between NYPD A-LT. and this author.

Sousa, W. H. (2010). Paying attention to minor offenses: Order maintenance policing in practice. Police Practice & Research, 11(1), 45-59. doi:10.1080/15614260802586

US DOJ. (1999). Promising strategies to reduce gun violence report. Washington DC: US Dept. of Justice.

Maritime Security and Piracy on the High Seas

✿ ✿ ✿

O verseas trade with countries like China, Vietnam, Singapore, and Malaysia, are a reason an overwhelming majority of America's goods come into the country via sea routes (Kraska, 2011, p. 37). The United States is highly dependent on the global movement of freight and cargo via the seas, and this has exposed American cargo and other ships to the global reach of piracy, which affects both the economic and security of American flagged ships or foreign ships coming to America. The circumstances that modern day pirates have put the shipping agencies and the law enforcement agencies into, have brought attention to the issue. What the United States and the world community has done to put a halt to it all is presented here.

The International Maritime Organization (IMO) has a lengthy definition of privacy which essentially says that "any illegal acts of violence or detention" on the high-seas, this includes robbery, constitutes piracy (IMO, 2017, para. 1). This definition originates from the 1982 United Nations Convention on the Law of the Sea (UNCLOS). Authorities say that sea going piracy is currently at its worse off the coast of Somalia and Yemen, which is the bodies of the Gulf of Aden and the Arabian Sea (IMO, 2017, para. 2).

Piracy in this context can mean anything from two armed men in a skiff who pursue and illegally board a small sailboat, to a large group of men who pursue and board a cruise ship or even a mega tanker. Pirates make demands which usually revolve around money. This can be demands for ransom where they hold a person(s) for a day or two, or up to several years. In the book, *Hostage: A Year at Gunpoint with Somali Pirates*, a middle-aged couple describe their plight, being held captive over a year in Somalia as they extorted their family and friends for ransom. (Chandler, Chandler, & Edworthy, 2012, p. 43) There has been several cases where pirates demanded tens and even hundreds of millions of dollars in ransom fees (Boyle, 2015, p. 281). Pirates do not always get the ransom paid to them, and delayed ransom has led to hostages being murdered (Scharf, Newton, & Sterio, 2015, p. 128).

For the most part, pirates are exclusively men, mostly young Muslim men. They come from a war-torn country (Somalia), which sits directly across from another war-torn country, Yemen. Somalia has had 30 years of civil war, dictators, and general unstableness which has created a society which leaves young men with a bleak future. The dictators and small groups (Davis, 2012, p. 162) have "carved out" a place where radicalized groups essentially run the country. In Senate testimony, Sen. Olympia J. Snowe (ME) stated to RADM Brian M. Salerno of the U.S. Navy, "One of the clear root causes of the piracy epidemic in the Gulf of Aden and off Somalia's Indian Ocean coast is the inherent instability of the Somali government" (US Senate, 2009, p. 48). Fishing had been the only industry, but in large part, that has been superseded by piracy. The United Nations (UN) attempted to help, but a radical Islamic element damaged the U.N.'s willpower. In the early 1990s the United States sent in Navy SEALs and Marines to take back the largest port and bring some stability to the country (ADST, 2014, p. 1). However, it did not take long before it became a quagmire that resulted in several American men being killed. In October 1993, the Battle of Mogadishu between American forces and Somali militants (and civilians) culminated in a U.S. Army Black Hawk helicopter getting shot down and three soldiers being killed (ADST, 2014, p. 1). That would be the last major attempt the Americans made to assist with nation building in Somalia. Near twenty years later the U.S. Navy is off the coast of Somalia, not intervening with their country's government, but trying to keep the armed Somali pirates at bay. Uncle Sam is keeping the sea channels open so that food can get through, as pirates are stealing food that was destined for their own people—rice and other foodstuffs that originated from Japan and Germany (Njuguna, 2009, p. 1). Not all piracy takes place near the coast, piracy is known to take place as far as 1,500 miles off shore (WSC, 2017, p. 1), where the pirates use a stolen large ship as a mother ship to launch small boats which can then hunt innocent civilian ships.

Somalia pirates can be quite aggressive. They have not only killed innocent civilians and crew members of ships, but have fired on many ships over the years. Because of this, many ships, either privately owned or ships of various navies, have a use of force policy which allows them to return fire against the pirates. The militaries of the world, seemingly have no issues with defending their ships from these robbers. The pirates offer little resistance in their 14 foot skiff, when a 200 or 300 hundred foot Navy cruiser is steaming by. American, China, Russia,

India, have all put shots on target and destroyed the aggressive Somali pirate boats which have gone up against some massive sea might (Kirk, 2011, p. 2). The military of different countries have lent a hand patrolling the waters off of Somalia in an attempt to keep the pirates at bay. These same navies have brought diplomacy up in their attempts at helping to settle the problem in Somalia. All of the leaders of these ships realize that it is not on the water where the problem originates, but in the ravages of Somalia where there is no credible government to lay control over the pirates who have a free run of the country, its ports and all of the Gulf.

Some of the international navy ships have conducted large-scale arrest operations, because piracy is not all about a small boat here and there. At one point, Somalis held 12 western tankers and merchant ships hostage, along with 290 sailors (Kirk, 2011, p. 3). One of the most well known hijackings by pirates was the U.S. ship Maersk Alabama which was pursued and occupied by a group of gun wielding Somalis (Boon, 2011, p. 470). The film was turned into a major Hollywood film which was the first film to bring piracy and the problems off the Somali coast to the public. After the rescue of the ship, it's Chief Engineer Michael Perry testified in front of the U.S. Senate that,

> The long-term comprehensive solution calls for a response both at sea and ashore. The root cause of piracy must be addressed internationally. There are hundreds of mariners being held hostage aboard pirated vessels across the world, and the U.S. Government's resources alone are not enough to fix the problem (US Senate, 2009, p. 36).

Self-defense among the private industry is not as clear cut as it is for naval vessels. Private shipping companies have been hiring heavily armed private security officers for their vessels, because they don't want to be captured, have lives be put at risk, or be captured. Piracy is more than a distraction, and keeping away from pirates is incredibly important. In recent years, pirates have shot, pursued or boarded Carnival cruise line ships, tankers, freighters, small and large yachts, and small sailboats. These ships need to be able to fight back , and so several years ago the IMO established a set of Best Management Practices for ships, this includes using razor wire on the hull, provide anti-climbing paint, employing fire hoses and utilizing other defensive infrastructure on ships (IMO, 2017, p. 1). They also approved armed officers on ships, who can shoot back at pirates. Many of these officers are former military veterans from countries around the world. While the use of armed security officers is effective, it is very expensive.

Conclusion

The official policy of the U.S. is to "continue to lead and support international efforts to repress piracy...[because] the world have [sic] long considered pirates to be universal enemies of mankind" (US Dept. of State, 2014, p. 2). Some of the solutions to piracy include a potential ban on ransom payment from the US, the UN or other country--the pirates simple do not get money. Increasing the rules of engagement to be aggressive against the pirates, sink their ships and arrest them when they can be arrested will also help. Other items include providing economic aid to countries that intervene with their pirates in an attempt to halt their ways. Providing infrastructure assistance to help build courts and prisons so Somalia can best deal with their criminals. Providing military assistance to help fight radical Islamic groups and take back control of pirate-controlled areas, and provide a blockade in-between the sea and countries three major ports (Kirk, 2011, p. 3).

References

ADST. (2014, September 2). From nation-building to black hawk down: U.S. peacekeeping in somalia. Retrieved July 31, 2017, from http://adst.org/2014/09/from-nation-building-to-black-hawk-down-u-s-peacekeeping-in-somalia/

Boon, K. (2011). Piracy and international maritime security. Oxford University Press.

Boyle, J. (2015). Blood ransom: Stories from the front line in the war against Somali piracy. Bloomsbury Publishing.

Chandler, P., Chandler, R., & Edworthy, S. (2012). Hostage: A year at gunpoint with Somali pirates. Chicago Review Press.

Davis, J. (2012). Terrorism in africa: The evolving front in the war on terror. Lexington Books.

IMO. (2017). Piracy and armed robbery against ships. Retrieved July 30, 2017, from http://www.imo.org/en/OurWork/Security/PiracyArmedRobbery/Pages/Default.aspx

International Maritime Bureau. (2017). Piracy & armed robbery prone areas and warnings. Retrieved July 17, 2017, from https://www.icc-ccs.org/index.php/piracy-reporting-centre/prone-areas-and-warnings

Kirk, M. (2011). Ending Somali piracy against American and allied shipping. DIANE Publishing.

Kraska, J. (2011). Contemporary maritime piracy: International law, strategy, and diplomacy at sea. ABC-CLIO.

Njuguna, A. (2009, February 13). Somali pirates release Japanese ship - The San Diego Union-Tribune. Retrieved July 31, 2017, from http://www.sandiegouniontribune.com/sdut-piracy-021309-2009feb13-story.html

Scharf, M. P., Newton, M. A., & Sterio, M. (2015). Prosecuting maritime piracy: Domestic solutions to international crimes. Cambridge University Press.

US Dept. of State. (2014). U.S. counter piracy and maritime security action plan. Retrieved July 24, 2017, from http://www.state.gov/t/pm/rls/othr/misc/255332.htm

US Senate. (2009, May 5). Piracy on the high seas: Protecting our ships, crews, and passengers. Retrieved July 31, 2017, from https://www.gpo.gov/fdsys/pkg/CHRG-111shrg51472/html/CHRG-111shrg51472.htm

WSC. (2017). Piracy | World shipping council. Retrieved July 31, 2017, from http://www.worldshipping.org/industry-issues/security/piracy

Is Technology Leading to Microbial Cross-Contamination and Pathogen Spread in the Airport Environment?

✿ ✿ ✿

It is not a far off assumption that members of the public are not washing their hands prior to or after boarding a commercial aircraft. However, new procedures such as the gate agent taking a mobile phone from a passenger, scanning it on an electronic boarding pass reader, then handing it back to the passenger, may mandate this at some point. It seems modern electronic boarding passes are openly causing cross-contamination of microorganisms between aircraft employees and the general public. And while environmental and human contamination related to microbial cross-contamination and pathogen spread in the airport space is not a commonly discussed topic, the question that needs to be asked, is, should it be a paramount concern for public health officials?[1]

Background

It's well known that direct skin to skin contact and/or passing something between two individuals is a way that microorganisms can cross-contaminate. While human hands are harbingers of bacteria and viruses (among normal flora), so too are inanimate objects. Combine this in a situation where infrequent hand washing is the norm (such as traveling through an airport), and this can evolve to a point where infection becomes inevitable. There is a definite change occurring at airports across the world, as paper boarding tickets are rapidly bring replaced by electronic boarding tickets on mobile phones.

Formerly, one would obtain a paper boarding pass and hold on to it until they walked up to the aircraft gate to board their plane. They would give the boarding pass to the gate agent, they'd scan it and return the stub. And while using a mobile phone to do the same thing (passing it back and forth) superficially sounds similar, the big difference is that bacteria grows differently on plastics vs. paper.

In ambient air, paper (either made of wood pulp or cotton fibers), is not a medium which stays moist for long. Inherently, both wood pulp and cotton fibers dry rapidly, this manifests as having a natural bacteriostatic effect. Materials which once wet from moisture (i.e. from perspiration of the hand or intimate moisture from the nose or mouth) will have the opposite effect—this includes mobile phones, which will also have natural skin oils among the moist mixture. Due to their plastic shell, cell phones are prone to the growth of biofilm, an assemblage of microorganisms that cannot be easily wiped off and exist in a polysaccharide suspension; this type of biological material is not easily removed by gentle rinsing. "Biofilm represents a problem" as it can contribute to infections in humans.[2]

A 2014 Time magazine article entitled, "Bacteria Thrive for Days on Airplanes" discussed how bacteria lived on fomites inside an airplane cabin. This included on seatback pockets for 8 days, leather seats 7 days, plastic window shades for 3 days, and plastic tray tables for 3 days.[3]

The Situation

What is occurring, is that as passengers line up to board the aircraft, they step up to the gate, hand their mobile phone to the gate agent who takes the mobile phone from the passenger, scan it across a laser-sensor (which reads the screen) and hands it back to the passenger. This interaction of the gate agent handing the passengers mobile phone—then taking the next passengers phone, and so on, is openly cross-contaminating all the phones on the aircraft.

"Due to their plastic shell, cell phones are prone to the growth of biofilm, an assemblage of microorganisms that cannot be easily wiped off..."

For the purposes of this discussion, we are not focusing the initial Transportation Security Administration (TSA) Credential Authentication Technology and Boarding Pass Scanning System (CAT/BPSS) scanners that are at the entrance of the security screening area. We are focusing on the airline boarding gate barcode readers that customers use right before stepping onto the jet way proximal to the aircraft. These are typical modern glass top readers which can interpret emailed 2D barcode boarding passes; these are commonly displayed on mobile phones and tablets. Austrian Airlines was the first airline to offer electronic boarding passes that could be pulled up on mobile phones in the mid-2000s,[4] today, these are in use around the United States and across the globe by most carriers.

Mobile phones are prone to being "dirty," and medical science has abundantly confirmed this. A 2012 study reported that mobile phones of health care workers are "potential vectors for transferring nosocomial pathogens" between patients and the community.[5] The results of this study demonstrated that out of 183 tested phones, 179 came back positive for bacteria, including Escherichia coli, MRSA and ESBL-producing E. coli.[6] In 2014, the Journal of Epidemiological Global Health reported on a study which 112 phones were swabbed and analyzed for bacterial colonization. Of the 112 phones studied, 94.6% were colonized with bacteria pathogens, including Staphylococcus Epidermidis, Bacillus spp., Staphylococcus aureus, Pseudomonas aeruginosa, Escherichia coli, and others.[7] A 2015 study found that mobile phones were reservoirs for the transmission of pathogens, and that out of a test group of 316 phones, 100% contamination was found.[8] Another study, this one in 2016, demonstrated that of 110 university student's phones that were tested, 77.3% of the phone were infected with Coagulase-negative staphylococci (CoNS) and Staphylococcus aureus.[9]

Summary

Inadequate hand hygiene may result in cross-transmission of pathogens and hand colonization or infection. Several studies have shown that microorganisms can survive on hands for differing times, and this may be from minutes to many hours. "Pathogens of fecal, nose or throat, and skin origin are most likely to be transmitted by the hands."[10] The literature clearly demonstrates that "contaminated hands could be vehicles for the spread of certain viruses and bacteria."[11] Handing someone a fomite such as a mobile phone which has spent much time in contact with someone's face and hands, then passing it back, is an assured way of transmitting microorganisms from one person to another. Cross-transmission of organisms by those with contaminated hands is heightened by variables such as moisture and the lack of handwashing.[12] What we realize is that examining environmental contamination related to microbial cross-contamination and pathogen spread (including the flu virus) in the airport space, should be a paramount concern for public health officials.[13] In late 2017, microbiological tests conducted at three major (non-disclosed) airports, demonstrated that the highest bacteria / fungal cell counts were located on the screens of self-service boarding pass kiosks, some 253,000 colony forming units (CFUs). This number is 2.5 times that of CFUs found on the airplane toilets, and 21.8 times higher than the number of CFUs found on the airplane's tray tables.[14]

Utilizing the current method to scan individual boarding passes: Hand-Phone-Hand (Scan) Hand-Phone-Hand presents a tangible risk that a number of opportunistic organisms (which may include bacteria, fungi and viruses) may be spread via the customers' mobile phones. This type of transmission may play a role in the development of subsequent microbial-related illnesses. The benefit of innovative technology that expedites the boarding of passengers, needs to be weighed against the potential for microbial cross-contamination and the potential, in some circumstances, for infection.

References

[1] Griffith CJ, et al. Environmental surface cleanliness and the potential for contamination during handwashing. American Journal of Infection Control. 2003;31:93–96.

[2] Balagna, C. et al., "Silver Nanocluster/Silica Composite Coatings Obtained by Sputtering for Antibacterial Applications" in Njuguna, James. (Ed.) Structural Nanocomposites: Perspectives for Future Applications. Springer: Aberdeen, UK. 2013. 226

[3] http://time.com/105453/bacteria-on-a-plane/

[4]http://www.itpro.co.uk/628036/ba-extends-mobile-boarding-passes

[5] Ustun C, Cihangiroglu M. Health care workers' mobile phones: a potential cause of microbial cross-contamination between hospitals and community. J Occup Environ Hyg. 2012;9(9):538-42.

[6] Ustun C. Op. cit.

[7] Nwankwo EO, Ekwunife N, Mofolorunsho KC. Nosocomial pathogens associated with the mobile phones of healthcare workers in a hospital in Anyigba, Kogi state, Nigeria. J Epidemiol Glob Health. 2014;4(2):135-40.

[8] Pal S, Juyal D, Adekhandi S, et al. Mobile phones: Reservoirs for the transmission of nosocomial pathogens. Adv Biomed Res. 2015;4:144.

[9] Kotris I, Drenjančević D, Talapko J, Bukovski S. Identification of microorganisms on mobile phones of intensive care unit health care workers and medical students in the tertiary hospital. Med Glas (Zenica). 2017;14(1):85-90.

[10] Greig, J.D. (2010). Infective doses and pathogen carriage. Public Health Agency of Canada. Food Safety Education Conference, Atlanta Georgia; 6.

[11] WHO Guidelines on Hand Hygiene in Health Care: First Global Patient Safety Challenge Clean Care Is Safer Care. Geneva: World Health Organization; 2009. 7, Transmission of pathogens by hands.

[12] WHO Guidelines on Hand Hygiene in Health Care. Op. cit.

[13] Griffith CJ, et al. Environmental surface cleanliness and the potential for contamination during handwashing. American Journal of Infection Control. 2003;31:93–96.

[14] Insurancequotes.com. Germs at the airport. (2018, January 12). Austin, TX.

An Influence on My Life in Emergency Management: Capt. Rodger D. Kelley, MD (1948-1992)

✧✧✧

In 1990 I was a young man who was a regular staff volunteer at the American Red Cross in Orange County, California on their disaster action team; I was a green EMT and loved to help out where I could. One day a white van pulled up and a man in an impressive dark blue jumpsuit uniform stepped out and went into the building. I quickly asked others who he was. I learned his name was Rodger Kelley, he was a physician, and was with the U.S. Public Health Service I was told. A few hours later I ran into him before he departed the parking lot and he engaged me in conversation; that brief encounter put me on a course which changed my life forever.

Captain Rodger D. Kelley, MD, was a former U.S. Naval officer and physician, that served in the Navy twice, first from 1973-1978, then again in the early 1990's during the Gulf War (USNR deployed with 4th Med Batt). There, he deployed to the field and treated combat casualties. Back home, Kelley helped bring together the U.S. Public Health Service (Office of the Assistant Secretary of Health / Office of Emergency Preparedness) and the American Red Cross, to create the first citizen-based emergency response team of the National Disaster

Medical System—the first Disaster Medical Assistance Team (DMAT). That team was founded in Orange County, California, and I was recruited by him to be a part of it. Our team trained and trained, we continually practiced and prepared for our mission, which was to supplement civilian communities after a disaster or attack by providing a medical response force. Being a part of that team led by Dr. Kelley was very satisfying, he often spoke about leadership, and how the country needed a better system to manage mass casualties, as the system they had at the current time was weak.

Then, in September 1992, I got the call—it was Dr. Kelley's Executive Officer telling me to get my go-bag and meet at 0400 at the Los Alamitos Army Airfield in preparation of deployment to Hawaii. That morning we would be responding with the US Public Health Service to support the State of Hawaii which had been struck by Hurricane Iniki. That deployment only lasted a week, but I was provided with experiences like none I had ever experienced. Dr. Kelley demonstrated and communicated leadership, pride, and a sense of duty to this 23-year-old. He tasked me to work with the FDA emergency teams to conduct potable water testing, to treat patients in a Kawaii field hospital, and to unpack and repack supplies—not because we wanted to do it, but because it had to be done. While in Hawaii, I found down time to chat with the doctor, and pick his brain, and learn some thoughtful lessons. He often spoke about leadership, including being a leader while dealing with emergencies, based on his personal experiences, that he picked up working in a combat theatre.

Several years later, I myself was in the leadership of a DMAT team in FEMA Region VIII. I was co-founder and served as Deputy Commander—the senior non-physician officer. After a couple of years, I was recruited by PHS officers from Rockville to help assemble a specialty WMD team, and served in that team's executive leadership. There, I provided guidance, direction, and supervision in the administrative operations and development of a federal emergency response team, and helped develop and implemented local strategies for building a highly visible National priority program, activities of the National Disaster Medical System. This included one of three specialty *National Medical Response Teams for Weapons of Mass Destruction* (NMRTWMDs).

Dr. Kelley was the influence who put me on the path which has led me to my career. From my experience in management with the USPHS and NDMS, I went on to have various opportunities in public safety. Today, I work full-time in corporate emergency management in New York City. Several years ago I joined the US Coast Guard Auxiliary where I remain active, and have served as a Vice-Flotilla Commander, and I'm currently exploring being part of a Coast Guard Incident Management Team.

My fellow team members and I didn't know it at the time, but Dr. Kelley came down with pneumonia on that fateful 1992 mission to Hawaii. Less than once month later, my mentor, and my friend, past away. An anonymous writer remarked in his obituary: "Dr. Kelley was a man on a mission. He was light years ahead of anyone else wanting—no, demanding—a national disaster response system. Time was not on his side." The doc was from San Clemente, California, where his ashes were scattered among the Pacific Ocean. Fair winds and following seas Dr. Kelley, you served your country in many ways, and all the ways were for the greater good of the nation.

About the Author

Shelomo Alfassa is a full-time corporate emergency management & homeland security professional in New York City. He has 25 years of public safety sector experience. He has served on several federal deployments on a joint US Public Health Service / FEMA CBRN counter-terrorism response team as Deputy Commander (G8 Summit, the Atlanta Olympics, etc.), and on major Hurricane responses with the *National Disaster Medical System.*

He is a member of the *International Association of Emergency Managers* (IAEM), and the *Section on Emergency and Crisis Management* of the *American Society for Public Administration* (ASPA). He's an active uniformed member of the *US Coast Guard Auxiliary*, and a vetted member of several 'First Responder Groups' for the US Department of Homeland Security, *Science & Technology Directorate.* He is a member of the "Electronic/Security Systems" sub-committee of ASTM International's Committee E54 on *Homeland Security Applications.* He is also a vetted member of the FBI *InfraGard* program and the author and editor of several non-fiction books on history.

Alfassa's formal education includes a Harvard Business School post-graduate Certificate in Sustainable Business Strategy; a BA in Homeland Security and a Masters in Public Administration from APU. He is a Certified Emergency Disaster Professional (CEDP), Facilities Security Officer (FSO 33 CFR § 105.205), an EMT (27 years). He has been a speaker at events such as the N.Y. State Emergency Managers Conference; ISC-EAST; and has appeared on Fox News, MSNBC, and PIX11, etc.

Index

www.ingramcontent.com/pod-product-compliance
Lightning Source LLC
Chambersburg PA
CBHW030744200526
45160CB00007B/11